SCHOOL HOUSE WRECK

JASON LINKINS
WITH
PHIL LEWIS

2018

WASHINGTON D.C.

Published in the United States by Strong Arm Press, 2018

www.strongarmpress.com

Book design and Composition by Strong Arm Press

Cover Art by Ebonie Land.

ISBN: 1-947492-05-5
ISBN-13: 978-1-947492-05-9

CONTENTS

DEDICATION AND ACKNOWLEDGMENTS

I am grateful to Ryan Grim, Alex Lawson and the whole team at Strong Arm Press for both roping me into doing this and making this such a wonderful experience. A huge helping of gratitude to Phil Lewis for stepping in with some amazing reporting. Thanks also to Rachel Cohen and Alex Abbott for lending their considerable editorial expertise.

Many people made sizable contributions toward getting this book where it is. Among them, debts are owed to Alexis Goldstein, Chris Lehmann, and Shahien Nasiripour.

Special thanks to my wife, Caroline -- a public school special education teacher -- for helping me, and obviously many others, who really need the help now more than ever.

SCHOOLHOUSE WRECK

Wouldn't have been possible without your help.

Like all our titles at Strong Arm Press, this book was funded by hundreds of donors who gave small amounts to make it happen. A handful of readers gave well above what we could ever reasonably expect from readers, and we wanted to thank them here:

Heidi Frey Greenwald
Allan Fix
Pamela Stanley
Brian Williams
Gay Charlton
Wayne Pearce
Jackie B. Duncan
Zak Linkins
Rhonda Weingarten
Mark Hurst
Margery Johnson
Karen Wehrman
Ruth A. Harnisch
Edward Baumgartner
Terry Maddox
Allan Greenleaf
Ray Bellamy

Visit StrongArmPress.com to find future projects you can help make a reality.

CHAPTER ONE: RECEIVE MODE

The first thing you notice about Betsy DeVos -- President Donald Trump's choice to run the United States Department of Education -- is that she is rich.

Actually, the word "rich" doesn't really do it justice. Cookie batter is rich. Betsy DeVos is wealthy in the way that Donald Trump wishes he was (and very well may be by the time his presidency is over).

Betsy DeVos is on another level entirely.

Begin with the family money. Before Betsy DeVos was a DeVos, she was a Prince -- the daughter of Edgar Prince, to be specific. Prince *pere* ran a successful auto parts manufacturing business in Holland, Michigan, which he had built into a billion-dollar empire by the time of his death. Prince used some of his personal wealth to bankroll what would become the organizational infrastructure of the religious right, providing vital seed money for conservative Christian advocacy groups like the Family Research Council and Focus on the Family. Betsy's brother Erik Prince would parlay his career as a Navy Seal into the founding of a private military contractor, formerly known as Blackwater. Blackwater's hired mercenaries, often driven by a Christian or at least anti-Muslim zeal, would invite such scandal upon the organization that we cannot really be sure what new name it's operating under by the time you pick up this book.

Betsy would follow a different path from her brother. Bringing about one of the largest mergers of conservative wealth, she married into the DeVos family, whose patriarch -- father-in-law Richard DeVos -- had built a multi-billion dollar fortune as the co-founder of multi-level marketing behemoth Amway.

That sort of money opens a lot of doors, many of which can be found on the collection of homes, helicopters, boats and planes that Betsy and her husband Dick own throughout the world. The couple's primary residence in Holland, Michigan, valued at $10 million, is a 22,000 square foot compound, built in 2010 on the site of the 12,000 square foot residence that was deemed to be insufficient.

And that's just the tip of the wealth-berg. Betsy and Dick have long been itinerant home collectors -- past acquisitions include a $2.4 million summer cottage overlooking Lake Michigan, another home in Vero Beach, Florida, and a chalet amid Colorado's tony slopes.

When it comes to transportation, the DeVoses need not be caught in first class, where they'd be forced to come near the public as the masses trudge with their carry-ons toward coach. They own at least three aircraft (including a Cessna Citation III, a Cessna Caravan, and a Cirrus SR-22), two helicopters, and ten boats -- including a 50-meter super-yacht named the Seaquest. According to Yacht Harbour's "superyacht database," DeVos and her family "have been linked to no less than 13 yachts over the years." These include two other fifty-meter mega-yachts, as well as a bevy of smaller vessels -- such as the 76-foot Reliance, on which Rich DeVos' grandson spent two years circumnavigating the globe. (Yacht Harbour notes that the DeVoses have a "solid preference for Westport yachts," and "may even have acquired a stake in the US yacht manufacturer.")

They also employ a small army of assistants to help their family with extremely basic things, including "a personal assistant to take care of all their Christmas season needs from suggesting gift ideas, buying gifts and wrapping presents," and a property manager who ensures that "doors are well-oiled to avoid squeaking."[1]

---

[1] Dupuy, B. (11 November 2017). VERY RICH BETSY DEVOS HAS 10 BOATS, TWO HELICOPTERS, A YACHT SCHEDULER AND A LAVISH LIFESTYLE YOU CAN'T AFFORD. *Newsweek.* http://www.newsweek.com/can-you-afford-betsy-devoss-lavish-lifestyle-708369

SCHOOLHOUSE WRECK

Taken as a whole, hers isn't merely the sort of wealth that renders one "out of touch" with the common man -- it's a fortune that has shielded DeVos from anything that even remotely resembles hardship from the time she was born until now. She has had no real contact or experience with adversity of any kind. She is almost a celestial body — untouched and untrammeled by the obstacles and pitfalls that the vast majority of the American people have to navigate on a daily basis.

And for that same vast American majority, education — and all of the mobility and opportunity it offers — is the primary vehicle by which they have to surmount the myriad challenges they face. It should be a matter of great concern that the person who now oversees America's educational infrastructure has never even nominally shared in these struggles.

Of course, with Betsy DeVos, the educational concerns don't end there. She has long yearned to radically transform public education, dramatically increasing the number of private and religious schools that educate American children. She's called U.S. public schools a "dead end" and in 2001, she explained how her school choice advocacy is driven by a desire to "advance God's kingdom." Aside from her ideological Christian fervor, she and her family also strongly support recreating schools in a more plutocratic image, where they can reward those entrepreneurial innovators looking to make a buck. When Trump tapped her to serve as his Education Secretary the public raised a hue and cry that even caught the liberal activists in the raise-a-hue-and-cry business by surprise.

Fittingly, however, DeVos' appointment has given her an illuminating first taste of what adversity actually feels like. During her second week on the job, she got a high-test dose of it in the form of a Twitter war -- which ended up being a microversion of her approach to the job, and her difficulty relating to the public and the teachers she ostensibly leads.

Twitter fights are, perhaps, to be expected. After all, this is the era of Donald Trump, for whom short bursts of id on America's premiere platform for sexual harassment and neo-Nazi cosplay are a regular feature. But long before her boss was escalating nuclear conflicts with North Korean dictators in brief pidgin English bursts from his unsupervised smartphone, DeVos had ended up in a conflict with less potential for bringing about the end of human civilization, this one with educators at the District of Columbia's Jefferson Middle School Academy. She had paid a visit to this school — in her first big public outing as the

3

head of the United States Department of Education — just a few days before.

DeVos' visit to Jefferson Academy did not go exactly as she would have liked. What might otherwise have been a trip that was barely worth mentioning instead drew viral attention after DeVos was greeted by a small rump of protesters. Bearing "Black Lives Matter" signs, the disgruntled assemblage, composed mainly of members of the Washington Teachers' Union, parents, and local activists, briefly impeded her as she tried to gain entry to the school. She was eventually escorted back to her waiting SUV, trailed by one agitant who chanted "Shame!" at her in the style of Game Of Thrones' Septa Unella. (It is perhaps lost on cultural dilettantes that Thrones' fans do not tend to identify positively with the Faith Militant -- in real life, such zealous foot soldiers would more easily identify with DeVos -- but it made for good video, nonetheless.)

It didn't take long for DeVos to gain entry into the school,[2] where a nervous staff of educators, "troubled by [her] decades-long campaign to promote vouchers as a way to escape public schools" and fearful that DeVos' presence was merely designed to furnish "a photo op to burnish her image," awaited her visit with no small amount of trepidation.

It's not like D.C.'s public schools are strangers to the occasional visit from glad-handing Secretaries of Education — the Obama administration had made good use of their proximity to this target-rich environment during its eight-year tenure. Still, as one Jefferson teacher told Brown, "Obama was not rooting against the very essence of what we are."

But when DeVos first emerged from her visit, she certainly didn't sound like someone rooting against Jefferson Academy. In a statement put out by the Department of Education[3], DeVos declared the school to be "a public middle school on the rise and a great example of the successful collaborative innovations occurring within the D.C. Public Schools system."

---

[2] Brown, E. (10 February 2017). Protestors briefly block Education Secretary DeVos's visit to a D.C. School. *The Washington Post.* https://www.washingtonpost.com/local/education/protesters-rally-at-dc-school-ahead-of-visit-by-education-secretary-betsy-devos/2017/02/10/faad4962-ef06-11e6-b4ff-ac2cf509efe5_story.html?utm_term=.d855cb6875a5

[3] U.S. Department of Education Press Office. (10 February 2017). Statement from U.S. Education Secretary Betsy DeVos on Visiting Jefferson Middle School Academy in Washington D.C. *U.S. Department of Education.* https://www.ed.gov/news/press-releases/statement-us-education-secretary-betsy-devos-visiting-jefferson-middle-school-academy-washington-dc

She continued:

> "Focusing on their students and families is at the heart of Jefferson Academy's approach, and that's exactly what I believe is at the heart of providing an exceptional education. Great teachers and leaders help make great schools, and I was honored to speak with Jefferson's team about our shared commitment to strengthening public education."

Now, DeVos didn't exactly stick her dismount. Another part of that statement, which mentioned the critics who greeted her outside and included the necessary sop to "respecting" peaceful protest, featured this admonition, "No school door in America will be blocked from those seeking to help our nation's school children" -- a tone-deaf addendum that seemed to liken the Secretary to Ruby Bridges, the first black child to integrate New Orleans' all-white William Frantz Elementary School in 1960. (Later, an equally tone-deaf editorial cartoonist would make this comparison explicit[4] with an image that parodied Norman Rockwell's 1964 painting, "The Problem We All Live With.")

Nevertheless, DeVos had turned her troubled start with Jefferson Academy into a more-or-less clean getaway -- with the emphasis on less, but still -- with praise properly rendered and bromides disseminated. Perhaps, it appeared, the awesome responsibility of her new position would change her as much as she hoped to change the system.

Or perhaps not. It's just not in DeVos' nature to leave well enough alone, and sure enough, she didn't. In a subsequent interview[5], she turned on the "great teachers" she had praised some days before:

> I visited a school on Friday and met with some wonderful, genuine, sincere teachers who pour their heart and soul into their classrooms and their students and our conversation was not long enough to draw out of them what is limiting them from being even more success from what they are currently. But I can tell the attitude is more of a 'receive mode.' They're waiting to be

[4] Sundby, A. (16 February 2017). Editorial cartoon comparing Betsy DeVos to Ruby Bridges defended by cartoonist. *CBS News.* https://www.cbsnews.com/news/editorial-cartoon-betsy-devos-ruby-bridges-defended-cartoonist/

[5] Thomas, C. (16 February 2017). Interview of Secretary of Education Betsy DeVos. *Townhall.* https://townhall.com/columnists/calthomas/2017/02/16/interview-of-secretary-of-education-betsy-devos-n2286164

told what they have to do, and that's not going to bring success to an individual child. You have to have teachers who are empowered to facilitate great teaching.

Well, Jefferson's staff were definitely not waiting to be told this, and they took to Twitter to answer back.

> This is what Sec. DeVos said about our teachers after her visit. Needless to say, we're about to take her to school. First, the secretary visited the classroom of Ashley Shepherd and Britany Locher, a dynamic co-teaching team that differentiates for the needs of students ranging from a first grade level to an eighth grade level in reading. They build amazing relationships with students and maintain a positive classroom environment focused on rigorous content, humor, and love. They aren't waiting to be told what to do.

> Then she saw Latisha Trent in action. Ms. Trent has been at Jefferson for 3 years, and each year her students grow MULTIPLE grade levels in Math. EVERY student realizes his or her maximum potential in Ms. Trent's room. She isn't waiting to be told what to do.

> Then the Sec. met Band teacher Jessica Harris, who has built our Music program from the ground up. Ms. Harris pours her heart into her work. Ms. Harris is patient, kind, relentless, and reflective. She is everything you want in a teacher. She isn't waiting to be told what to do.

> Morgan Markbreiter was there as well. Ms. MB has unleashed the passion of countless students through her Video Game Design course. MB also runs our INCREDIBLE after-school program, which provides FREE tutoring and enrichment to our kids. She isn't waiting to be told what to do.

Jefferson's Twitter spokesperson ended with a flourish: "JA teachers are not in a 'receive mode.' Unless you mean we 'receive' students at a 2nd grade level and move them to an 8th grade level."

It was, as the kids say, a "savage own." DeVos was forced to offer something of a meek recantation, responding to Jefferson Academy on Twitter, "Your teachers are awesome! They deserve MORE freedom to innovate and help students. Great teachers deserve freedom and flexibility, not to constantly be on the receiving end of government dictates."

All in all, it was an amusing, if common chapter in the life of a government factotum. Beyond the fact that all of this went down during DeVos' "soft launch" as Education Secretary after a shocking Senate confirmation process where the billionaire philanthropist admitted she wasn't familiar with the federal statute protecting students with disabilities, this story is nothing much beyond an administration official meeting with a little adversity on the way to a photo-op and offering up some ill-considered banter in an interview after the fact.

There is, however, a moment in all of this that's worth a closer examination -- and that's DeVos' specific charge, that the teachers she met, like teachers across the country, are passive, waiting idly by until they receive marching orders from on high, and stuck in a holding pattern, to the detriment of students. It seemed almost unfathomable that she'd look to sow such unnecessary ill-will within a fortnight of being anointed to federal power.

But where would DeVos be today without her steadfast belief that she knows better than anyone else working in education today? Throughout the course of her long career, she has sought to foist her particular ideological rubric upon every school system onto which she could get her hands, and has underwritten a similar effort on those school systems that remained, frustratingly, just out of her immediate reach. If anything, she should be delighted to encounter teachers in "receive mode" — supplicants awaiting her lofty commandments. In a sense, DeVos was lambasting the very qualities she has always depended on others to have.

Indeed if there's one thing that Betsy DeVos has been good at doing, it's fomenting bad blood. Parents, especially those with high-needs children, don't trust her[6]. Many veteran school choice acolytes, who one might imagine would identify a kindred spirit in her well-worn

[6] Brown, E. (4 February 2017). The popular uprising that threatens the Betsy DeVos nomination. *The Washington Post*. https://www.washingtonpost.com/local/education/the-popular-uprising-that-threatens-the-betsy-devos-nomination/2017/02/03/bd7c19aa-e967-11e6-80c2-30e57e57e05d_story.html?utm_term=.70e175cfa027

pontifications, have been loath to embrace her[7] -- in part because her own Michigan "school choice" experiments have proven to be abysmal failures.[8] And at the end of her confirmation process, the Trump White House had to send Vice President Mike Pence over to the Senate to cast a tie-breaking vote because there weren't even enough Republicans willing to sign their names on the dotted line. (Not to mention that five Republicans on the Senate Committee on Health, Education, Labor, and Pensions had received more than $250,000 from DeVos and her family.)

If there's been one constant during DeVos' time in Donald Trump's orbit -- from the day he first named her as his pick to lead the Department of Education, to the autumn of her first year on the job -- it's been her unpopularity. It's not for nothing that NPR's Anya Kamenetz published a piece titled, "How Betsy DeVos Became Trump's Least Favorite Cabinet Pick" just after Groundhog Day, and HuffPost's Amanda Terkel was able to follow suit with her own piece, headlined "How Betsy DeVos Became The Most Hated Cabinet Secretary" in the run-up to Halloween. Sandwiched between those bookends was a Politico/Morning Consult poll, conducted in September, that found that DeVos was -- yes -- the least-liked member of Trump's cabinet. Truly, DeVos is to popularity as Sisyphus is to rolling stones up an incline.

Those who have had the opportunity to measure the public's dislike of DeVos typically speak as though they were in awe, that the backlash wasn't something they would have ordinarily anticipated. "She's very, very polarizing," said one GOP official who helped with her confirmation process. "It's amazing, because she's incredibly nice and harmless in person. But there's just something about her." Heidi Hess, who runs campaigns for the good-government organization CREDO Action, told NPR's Kamenetz that "nobody has gotten people as enraged as DeVos," and that the outpouring of opposition has "smashed CREDO's record for petition signatures."

"A million and a half is just unprecedented," she told Kamenetz. "It's another scale of magnitude."

---

[7] Brown, E. (12 December 2016). School choice advocates divided over Trump and his education pick, Betsy DeVos. *The Washington Post.*
https://www.washingtonpost.com/local/education/school-choice-advocates-divide-over-trump-and-his-education-pick-betsy-devos/2016/12/09/6c377824-b806-11e6-b8df-600bd9d38a02_story.html?utm_term=.7cda791c7a93
[8] Emma, C. Benjamin, W. (9 December 16). DeVos' Michigan schools experiment gets poor grades. *Politico.* https://www.politico.com/story/2016/12/betsy-devos-michigan-school-experiment-232399

And as Terkel reported in November, that disapproval was still sky-high months later. According to a HuffPost/YouGov poll conducted in early October, DeVos was still the most unpopular cabinet member, alongside Attorney General Jeff Sessions, with a 42 percent unfavorability rating. DeVos and Sessions also tied one another among those who were asked about what cabinet members were doing "a bad job," at 32% each. It's really no wonder that DeVos was taking star turns in the often dire-sounding fundraising missives with which Democratic campaigns bombard unsuspecting email inboxes. As one Democratic operative told HuffPost, communiques that feature DeVos "tend to perform very strongly."

And yet, this phenomenon can puzzle the casual observer. As federal agencies go, the Department of Education really doesn't attract a lot of media attention, and its secretaries are among the least powerful cabinet positions. And DeVos herself is widely said to be friendly and collegial in person.

Even in the Trump administration, which has an unhealthy obsession with constantly making news, Betsy DeVos isn't being regularly dragged into the harsh light of the media kliegs. Instead, she has earned her enmity the hard way.

Sessions' relative unpopularity doesn't come as a surprise -- he's long been at the center of Trump's ethno-nationalist hustle, as well as playing a leading role in the ongoing, ever-expanding investigations into the Trump inner circle's dealings with Russian officials.

Treasury Secretary Steven Mnuchin and (the quickly scuppered) Health and Human Services Secretary Tom Price have been similarly present in our consciousness as key players in two important White House policy initiatives, tax reform and the repeal of the Affordable Care Act. And the Department of Education, under DeVos, has not been the subject of deep-dive reporting on how the agency has devolved into a harrowing welter of dysfunction and grave worry, as have been written about Rex Tillerson's State Department and Rick Perry's Department of Energy.

Even that vaunted satiric tribune of our times, Saturday Night Live -- flush with Emmys over their recent, politics-infused seasons -- couldn't do much with DeVos. Kate McKinnon made one game stab at playing the character and never returned to it.

All of which is to say, it can seem remarkable at first, given how many different Trump administration flunkies have occupied the media's attention, to find DeVos so firmly -- and so negatively -- planted in the consciousness of Americans.

It certainly has been a surprise to DeVos. In March 2018, she sat down for an ill-advised interview with 60 Minutes, part of an ill-advised media tour aimed, apparently, at reminding people that Betsy DeVos is still around.

"Why have you become, people say, the most hated Cabinet secretary?" Leslie Stahl wanted to know.

"I'm not so sure exactly how that happened. But I think there are a lot of really powerful forces allied against change," ventured DeVos.

"Does it hurt?" Stahl wanted to know.

"Sometimes it does. Sometimes it does. Again, I think — I think — I'm more misunderstood than anything."

It could be, however, that DeVos is understood perfectly well, producing a legitimate consensus that has emerged from Americans' elemental understanding of the importance of education itself. Education is not an abstraction. We have all lived it, or are living it.

The notion of good schooling being the central force behind societal change and individual advancement has long been a part of our frontier mythology. It's every family's calling to leave their offspring better off than their antecedents, and education has long been an important means to that end. As sociologist Tressie McMillan Cottom puts it in her book, Lower Ed, education in America is a gospel. For better or for worse, it sells salvation. And in its finest moments, it can really lift people from desperation to prosperity.

But, as Cottom would tell you, not all of its moments are fine, and not all of its avatars are clad in priestly vestments. Televangelists also stalk the land, profiting from this desperation, preying upon the desperate, and propping up their con so that this grift can be repeated. Betsy DeVos fits well within this coterie of charlatans. But she also stands out among them, in ways that are impossible not to notice, and what people see leaves many concerned about the future of public schools -- which are still widely cherished in America.

DeVos' family boodle greases the machinery throughout the conservative landscape -- their family foundation is a major donor to right-wing organizations like the American Enterprise Institute, the Heritage Foundation, the Family Research Council, ALEC's State Policy Network, and FreedomWorks, just to name a few.

Betsy DeVos' devotion to the crass and opaque political donor infrastructure wrought by our loose control of oligarchical influence in our politics and the Supreme Court decisions that have propped up this regime is absolute and long-standing. Back in 1997, she made her position clear in a Roll Call op-ed, where she said she has "decided to stop taking offense at the suggestion that we are buying influence. Now I simply concede the point. They are right. We do expect something in return." By her own accounts, she was at the time the biggest contributor of soft money to the Republican National Committee. She's since become a dark-money dealer as well.

There's a straight line from DeVos' bank accounts[9] to legislative pushes for legally enshrined discrimination. In 2015, for example, in her home state of Michigan, her family funded a campaign for the adoption of a statewide "religious freedom restoration act" (RFRA), which would have sanctioned discrimination against Michigan's LGBTQ community. Her money also underwrote the passage of what came to be known as "the death star" -- HB 4052, a "state pre-emption" law that banned municipalities from making autonomous decisions about wages and benefits. DeVos' money also funded the Mackinac Center for Public Policy, from which emerged the new "emergency manager" regime that swept across Michigan, stealing lawmaking power from duly elected officials and placing it firmly in the hands of unaccountable political appointees. It was this arrangement that led, directly, to the lead water crisis in Flint, Michigan.

DeVos' primary devotion has been the slow-motion annihilation of public schools. She has long been a fierce proponent of privatizing as much of America's public education system as she can, spending her monetary and political capital on any number of "school choice" schemes that would prop up private, religious, and charter schools. To that end, she's generously feathered the nests of such 501(c)(4) groups as the American Federation for Children and the Alliance for School Choice, which have in turn pushed for school vouchers, privatization and all that comes with it -- such as the funneling of public money into the hands of unaccountable private corporations, and the degradation of teacher unions and labor rights.

"School choice," sold by DeVos as a curative to widening economic inequality, is actually a product of that inequality. It shouldn't be lost on anyone that school vouchers pair well with "pre-emption" laws that

---

[9] Strauss, M. (1 December 2015). Who Was Behind Michigan GOP's One-Two Punch Against LGBTQ Working Families? *Political Research Associates*.
http://www.politicalresearch.org/2015/12/01/end-of-a-tough-year-for-michigan-who-was-behind-the-one-two-punch-from-gop-lawmakers/#sthash.Czw94OoK.Yf5ld4gU.dpbs

prevent municipalities from raising their minimum wage -- they provide the comforting illusion that economic mobility and equality is still possible in a world where policy choices are compounding wage stagnation. Nor is it coincidental that DeVos has spent a sizable fortune in an effort to bolster religious schools while also fanatically devoting herself to undermining the rights of the LGBTQ community. (Every time DeVos is asked about whether private schools that discriminate against gay students should be allowed to receive federal funds, she evades answering.)

That said, DeVos has found her vision to be a tough sell -- even to similarly minded advocates of charter schools and voucher systems. A big reason why is that her effort to transform Michigan's education system to her liking was such a notable failure. As Politico's education team reported in December of 2016, after twenty years of unrestrained charter school growth in Michigan, "the state's overall academic progress has failed to keep pace with other states," and "the state's charter schools scored worse on that test than their traditional public-school counterparts." And that's just the start of Michigan's woes. Per Politico:

> Critics say Michigan's laissez-faire attitude about charter-school regulation has led to marginal and, in some cases, terrible schools in the state's poorest communities as part of a system dominated by for-profit operators. Charter-school growth has also weakened the finances and enrollment of traditional public-school districts like Detroit's, at a time when many communities are still recovering from the economic downturn that hit Michigan's auto industry particularly hard.

> The results in Michigan are so disappointing that even some supporters of school choice are critical of the state's policies.

As the Politico reporters note, the DeVoses' "influence can be seen in just about every major piece of education-related legislation in Michigan since the 1990s."

Beyond the failing grades of DeVos' enacted vision, it's hard for ordinary people to not grasp her fraudulence. DeVos boasts no formal training in pedagogy or curriculum design, and shows no evidence of policy knowledge beyond the free-market fundamentalism her family has embraced since birth. She has never worked in a public school, attended a public school, or even sent any of her own children to one. And in her aggravatingly hypocritical style, she once lambasted her "school choice" critics for sending "their own children to prestigious private schools." (However, one barb that she is continually dogged with, that she's never even set foot in a public school, *is* an unfair and untrue criticism -- a glib talking point that her opponents have managed to make stick.)

Nevertheless, the single biggest divide between DeVos and most ordinary Americans is that most people love their public schools. As NPR's Kamenetz reported during her foray into DeVos' unpopularity, "national polls consistently show that a majority of Americans, across the aisle, approve of their neighborhood schools,"[10] even when their opinions of education, writ large, aren't particularly glowing. What's more, Kamenetz notes, is that they "oppose closing them down[11], even when they are low-performing."

And when DeVos flounders on basic questions about public education, as she continually did during her Senate confirmation hearing, it only reaffirms the already widely held perception that she is fantastically out of her depths.

It might seem like the fear that Betsy DeVos could revamp public schools as the Secretary of Education is mistaken. After all, the Department of Education doesn't really have the power to take DeVos' failed Michigan "school choice" fantasia nationwide. Those decisions are made at the state and local level. But those who dismiss the fear out of hand are not understanding the threat in the right way. Betsy DeVos did not become the Secretary of Education to radically transform public schools. Rather, it is her constant promotion of the radical transformation of public schools, combined with her fulsome funding of conservative politicians and think-tanks, that paved her way to this plum appointment. In doing so, it's incentivized the furtherance of DeVos' schemes by those who'd want to follow a similar career path.

At some point, DeVos' time in Washington will end, and from there, she'll be able to pursue her radical "school choice" agenda bearing the imprimatur of a former Secretary of Education. In the meantime, however, she can use her powerful perch to wreak many different sorts

---

[10] Kamenetz, A. (23 August 2016). Americans Like Their Schools Just Fine But Not Yours. *NPR.* https://www.npr.org/sections/ed/2016/08/23/490380129/americans-like-their-schools-just-fine-but-not-yours

[11] Kamenetz, A. (23 August 2016). Americans Like Their Schools Just Fine But Not Yours. *NPR.* https://www.npr.org/sections/ed/2016/08/23/490380129/americans-like-their-schools-just-fine-but-not-yours

of harm. In fact, it hasn't taken her very long to unleash a parade of horribles. In less than a year, DeVos has undone student loan protections, scuttled the Department's sexual assault policy, rescinded guidelines that enumerated the rights of students with disabilities, and propped up the shady doings of scam-ridden for-profit colleges.

DeVos' comical ignorance of the realm she seeks to lead may occasionally find itself on glaring display, but a knowing scheme has nevertheless emerged. DeVos' preferred policies serve to benefit her plutocratic cronies and ideological fellow-travelers while unravelling whatever thin skein of protections exist for the most vulnerable. Once this pattern is identified, it becomes more clear why DeVos' popularity has slipped below that of the Trump administration's better-known clowns. As the Huffington Post's Terkel summarized, "In the Trump Cabinet, it turns out, you can more or less get away with being a plutocrat, a dilettante, or a saboteur hostile to the very mission of the agency you mean to lead. You just can't get away with being all three at once."

The problem is, despite public opinion, maybe she can.

CHAPTER TWO: MICHIGAN

Born on January 8, 1958, Betsy Prince was almost assuredly destined to be something of a major player in politics, just on the strength of her father Edgar's billion-dollar auto-parts business and his keen interest in Christian, conservative politics.

Betsy and her brother Erik were first-generation billionaire. Edgar had grown up poor, his own father having died when he was young. "All through high school, Edgar worked, most of the time for a car dealer," said a high school friend of Edgar's. The friend knew Edgar up until the day he died, but he didn't want to be named in this book, given how controversial the family is back home. "Edgar needed to make money to help support his family," he said, explaining that the Prince family had been active in the local Christian Reformed Church, which had its own school, but Edgar went to public school because his family couldn't afford the private alternative.

"The reason he did not go to a Christian school of his denomination was because it costs money and they obviously did not have a scholarship program that allowed him to go there. So he went to the public school," he said. "He was very bright and had an exceedingly precise mind. A very precise mind. After high school, he went on to engineering college -- he must have received a significant scholarship to go to college because he had no money."

The Christian Reformed Church was formed in the late 19th Century in reaction to the Dutch Calvinist Church, which they found too liberal. "They try to live their lives and believe that life is ordered by the scriptures, which are the untarnished truth come from God. That's the background in which she was born and raised," he said. "So when people talk about her as being too Christian for today's secular world, it's out of that background."

Edgar married a fairly well off member of the church, Elsa, and toiled for nearly two decades before his business finally took off. But it was Betsy's marriage to Dick DeVos that truly accelerated her rise into and cemented her place within America's upper-most echelon of wealth and political influence. In order to understand the fearsome fullness of Betsy DeVos' manifestation into our lives, you have to first understand the DeVos family business: Amway.

Founded in 1959, Amway (the abbreviated form of American Way Association) was the brainchild of Betsy's father-in-law, Richard DeVos, and his long-time business partner Jay Van Andel. The two men were a pair of schoolyard chums who'd spent the better part of their lives together, brewing up entrepreneurial ideas. By 1949, the two men had repositioned their old Ja-RI Corporation into a distributorship for the Nutrilite brand of food supplements. A decade later, they broke out on their own and, with the best distributors in their Nutrilite network, brought Amway into being.

Amway's beginnings were about as modest as you can imagine. DeVos and Van Andel's first big move was to purchase the rights to manufacture and sell a laundry detergent named "Frisk" from its down-on-his-luck inventor. Renamed "Liquid Organic Cleaner" -- or "LOC," in the company's parlance -- this household good would become the first of many products poached by DeVos and Van Andel and brought into the company's empire. Some of its more notable wares include Dish Drops dishwashing liquid, the Artistry cosmetic brand, the eSpring water filter, and XS Energy drinks.

Now, if you're sitting there, wondering how it is that you've never heard of these products, that's because you're never going to run into them at the local Target or Walgreens. The animating idea behind Amway is that they aren't actually selling *products*, they're selling their own specific version of what's known as a multi-level marketing scheme, and dressing it up as a unique entrepreneurial opportunity in which anyone can play a part.

If you've been so fortunate as to have a friend involved in Amway, you've likely gotten the Amway pitch straight from their mouths. They want to cut you in on a unique opportunity to "be your own boss" and make a tidy sum of income just by "sharing with friends," eventually becoming financially independent -- even independently wealthy, if you play your cards right. Amway essentially markets a dream: a shot at getting out of the rat race and forging one's own path to prosperity using nothing but one's charm and rugged individualism.

But beneath these gauzy promises, Amway's machinations are a lot more grotty. Individuals are drafted into the Amway family, essentially becoming independent franchisees of Amway's product line. New recruits can purchase Amway's products from what the company bills as its wholesale price point. From there, the individual may use the products themselves, or resell them to others at a marked-up price. Depending on how much each franchisee purchases from the Company, or sells at a mark-up, they become eligible for certain bonuses. It's the least Amway can do, seeing as how their army of individual distributors are providing the company with de facto retail and marketing services.

But those recruited into Amway's system are encouraged to do much more than simply schlep their product line around, looking to find customers. For these individual franchisees, the real rewards come when they build their own network of distributors. Once they start succeeding in reeling in fresh bodies, the potential for profit increases dramatically, as the original franchisee is entitled to a cut of his ersatz salesforce's own profits. But the fun doesn't end there! Each person recruited into one of these arrangements receives similar encouragements to go forth and multiply for themselves, adding new downstream layers to the original franchisee's empire -- and cutting the original entrant into further profits.

To use Amway's terminology, what every individual knit up in this arrangement is trying to do is to create what's known as a "downline." The deeper the downline, the greater potential there is for profits at the top of the chain -- and in fact, one of the big selling points of the Amway lifestyle is this constantly hinted-at but never explicitly promised idea that after a brief and furtive period of hardcore recruiting, the person at the top of the pile gets to live easy -- after all, they're supposed to have a small army of sellers beneath them doing the bulk of the actual "work." (Those at the top of the chain also have the unique opportunity to sell a full-range of Amway branded materials, offering tips and tricks to selling and recruiting, to their downlines as well.)

And anyone making an Amway pitch can rightfully claim to be letting the next newbie in on the "ground floor" of a profitable enterprise because the whole point of Amway is to continually define the "ground floor" downward. Typically, Amway's representatives are far more relentless at selling the scheme than they are about selling dish detergent

-- as anyone who's ever found themselves sitting next to an Amway salesperson at a bar can probably attest.

Matt Roth, who detailed his own experiences living the Amway life [12] in the September 1997 issue of The Baffler, explains the distinctions of this business model like so:

> Imagine that you've struck a deal with a company to give you discounts for buying in bulk: If you buy $100 worth of stuff, they'll send you a 3 percent rebate. For $300 or more, it goes up to 6 percent, $600 or more, 9 percent, and so on up to $7,500 and 25 percent. Now, let's say you're unable to spend more than $100 a month, but manage to get seventy-four other people to go in with you. Together, you spend $7,500 and divide up the 25 percent rebate. Everyone saves money, and the rebate is shared equally. That's the idea behind a consumer co-op or wholesale buying club.
>
> Now, let's say you get the 25 percent rebate from the company but tell the other seventy-four participants, "Look, you've each spent only $100, so you'll get only a 3 percent rebate." Not only would you save 25 percent on your purchases, but you make a 22 percent profit on everyone else's. That's the idea behind Amway.

As Roth notes, this essentially means that Amway is "disguising [an] upward flow of fees within a downward flow of commissions" within each of these varied networks. And if you've started to get the sense that there's something inherently paradoxical about this business -- that eventually you have to run out of people to bring into a downline, that at some point someone is going to get mired in an unprofitable ground floor with no way of advancing -- Roth explains that this is baked into Amway's business model: the company's "high dropout rate...actually serves to keep the pool of potential distributors large."

"In other words," writes Roth, "Amway's salvation is its high rate of failure."

---

[12] Roth, M. (September 1997). Dreams Incorporated. *The Baffler.*
https://thebaffler.com/salvos/dreams-incorporated#fn7

Perhaps, right about now, there is a growing voice inside your head screaming, "This is nothing more than a pyramid scheme!" Indeed, through the years Amway has been occasionally battered with this accusation, but has managed to skate by without any sort of irreparable harm being done to their core business. As Roth notes, "A 1979 Federal Trade Commission investigation concluded that Amway was not in fact a pyramid scheme—only that some of its claims to prospective distributors were overly optimistic—because most of its revenue came from sales of actual products." In this way, Amway has managed to distinguish itself from other pyramid schemes. Unlike, for example, Bernie Madoff's scam investment fund -- in which his "downline" equivalents were investors unwittingly rooked into providing the cash necessary to cover his promised investment returns to upstream investors -- every participant in Amway's multilevel marketing arrangement simply looks like buyers and sellers making perfectly rational consumer choices.

Ultimately, the proof of Amway's vision is in the pudding. From their modest beginnings, Amway has become a global behemoth. Even in its leaner years, the company takes home substantial profits -- in 2015, a down year, it made $9.5 billion in sales. Richard DeVos now has an estimated net worth of $5.1 billion dollars and is frequently found on the lists of the world's most wealthy men.

But Amway has been much more than a mere bankroll to serve the DeVos family's means and ends. The foundational ideas that shaped the company have also shaped the DeVoses' worldview and have informed the way they've operated within it. Amway's overarching ethos of strict hierarchies, community connection, Calvinist morality, and long-view planning permeates everything the DeVos family does. These Amway-bred values and vision have enabled them to forge a formidable and spectacularly successful political dynasty.

Despite the fact that the DeVos family have achieved a level of wealth that could easily allow generation after generation of descendants to live a carefree existence, being a member of the DeVos family is no casual matter. They are tight-knit and heavily organized, living within a sort of enforced super-structure that has allowed this sprawling family to pursue their philanthropic and political ambitions with single-minded zeal and stunning success.

Richard DeVos, the de facto don of the clan, wrote about the unique way his family organizes itself for maximal impact in his 2014 memoir[13],

---

[13] Stanton, Z. (15 January 2017). How Betsy DeVos Used God and Amway to Take Over Michigan

19

Being Rich. In that tome, DeVos describes how the family's wealth and influence is directed by a "Family Council" -- comprised of Richard's children and their spouses. This "Family Council" actually operates from a "family constitution," and they meet on a regular basis to make key decisions on how and why to spend the family fortune. Beneath this governing body, the DeVos family also has what they call a "Family Assembly," into which Richard's grandchildren are inducted at age 16, "in a formal ceremony that everyone attends." At the age of 25, the grandchildren are permitted to vote on family matters, when "they have met additional qualifications for taking on this added responsibility."

The structure is very much akin to Amway's sprawling network of "uplines" and "downlines," but without the welter of chaos that consumes Amway's individual franchisees. As Zack Stanton reported in his deep dive into DeVos family doings in Politico:

> This family-government approach has so far enabled the DeVos family to avoid the public schisms and disagreements that have plagued other multigenerational dynasties. Any dissent is hashed out in private, and that enables the family to focus its collective efforts with the precision of a scalpel and the power of a chainsaw.

Stanton notes that the same blend of Calvinist theology and free-market evangelism that Amway's employees are steeped in permeate the DeVos family's doings as well. As Richard DeVos wrote in his 1975 book, "Believe!: The dynamic principles of success and fulfillment through steadfast belief in ... Human dignity .. Free enterprise .. America under God" (which, at the time of this writing was available at Amazon for a very reasonable $859.82), "The real strength of America is its religious tradition...Too many people today are willing to act as if God had nothing whatsoever to do with it. ... This country was built on a religious heritage, and we'd better get back to it. We had better start telling people that faith in God is the real strength of America!"

One thing that Betsy Devos' most ardent defenders and most dogged critics have in common, is that they all agree that the faith in which she's been steeped has shaped her worldview. Her own upbringing in the Christian Reformed Church -- a sect of true believers who believe

---

Politics. *Politico Magazine.* https://www.politico.com/magazine/story/2017/01/betsy-dick-devos-family-amway-michigan-politics-religion-214631

that life is ordered through Biblical scriptures, the unvarnished word of God -- has rooted her in a faith that was only magnified by years of Christian education. It's long been her desire to breach the church-state wall in education -- she makes no bones about it.

As John Austin, the director of the Michigan Economic Center puts it:

> One authentic, historic concern the Devoses have had about schools has been, "Why are our public schools the center of community life?" They would prefer that the church be the center of community life. So their interest in supporting private and religious schools has won their authentic interest and they would rather help the church and Church-based education be a center of life.

Making the best case for their family's own religious traditions, the DeVoses are far from being tight-fisted Scrooges with their money. On the contrary, they've long been among Michigan's top agents of philanthropy. Their footprint in Grand Rapids is so vast that almost nobody who's written about the vast array of things named after the DeVoses in that city has been able to avoid making the observation that they've all but displaced President Gerald Ford as Grand Rapids' most famous native.

In January of 2016, after years of inquiry, Forbes finally got to report the extent to which the DeVoses had served as Western Michigan's philanthropic angels -- approximately $1.2 billion in giving over the family's history. All that largesse found many homes[14] in the Western part of the state and in Grand Rapids in particular -- youth sports programs, art institutions, and Christian non-profit organizations that served the neediest populations all received significant support from the DeVos family's array of foundations. The Grand Rapids public schools system could count themselves the beneficiary of $2.6 million of DeVos generosity.

And all this giving has helped the DeVos family earn a lot of clout and goodwill in Western Michigan, whose residents tend to hold the family in higher regard than their fellow Michiganders to the east. As Gleaves Whitney, the director of the Hauenstein Center for Presidential Studies at Grand Valley State University told Politico[15], "The political narrative

---

[14] Martinez, S. (4 January 2016). How and why Amway's DeVos family gives away billions. *Michigan Live*. http://www.mlive.com/business/west-michigan/index.ssf/2016/01/devos_family_donations.html

[15] Stanton, Z. (15 January 2017). How Betsy DeVos Used God and Amway to Take Over Michigan

that has grown around [the family] is unfair...They have made life better for a lot of people, and I can't say that loudly enough."

But the DeVoses have also used that money, over time, to establish a beachhead for their particular brand of free-market fundamentalism. And while they cannot be credited for inventing the prosperity gospel, they have gone a long way to perfecting it -- and in so doing, they've made searing changes to Michigan's political landscape, not all of which can be said to have "made life better" for Michigan residents.

As Jennifer Berkshire describes in the February 2017 issue of The Baffler, Richard DeVos' Amway empire started to "hit its stride" in his home state of Michigan during the 1970s. The rate at which DeVos' company recruited more and more Michiganders into its ranks rivaled the massive union organizing that shaped Michigan's politics and economy for the better part of the preceding decades. The DeVos family was thus emerging as a key player in the cold war between labor and capital. "Beneath the family's pieties," writes Berkshire, the Devoses were "a familiar archetype":

> They're rabid anti–New Dealers whose crusade against the nanny state has never ceased. Western Michigan, a land of tulips and fine-grained religious disputes, is like nowhere else, but its right-wingers want what right-wingers across the land have wanted since the days of the DuPonts: freedom—from regulations that hamstring, taxes that confiscate, government that overreaches, and unions, above all unions, that gum up the whole profit-making works.

The DeVos family did little to deter the notion that they had envisioned a key role for themselves as field marshals in the ranks of the capital class. Richard DeVos steadily provided key players in the conservative movement, such as Focus On The Family and the American Enterprise Institute, with seed money. He and his business partner, Van Andel, were regular contributors to the Heritage Foundation's Policy Review journal, extolling the virtues of the *laissez-faire* marketplace in pieces that scolded government intervention in markets and which decried unions as anti-American.

Politics. *Politico Magazine.* https://www.politico.com/magazine/story/2017/01/betsy-dick-devos-family-amway-michigan-politics-religion-214631

Amway's success earned Van Andel a top perch at the U.S. Chamber of Commerce, and by the mid-1990s the company had emerged as one of the Republican Party's biggest sources of income. In October of 1994, Amway injected $2.5 million into the Republican National Committee's coffers -- the largest single donation to a political party for a single election cycle ever recorded.

And while other Republican mega-donors consume the lion's share of the media's attention, the DeVos family may have had a greater influence on the way campaign finance business gets done today. As Zack Stanton relates in Politico[16], the DeVoses' inside-outside game, in which they successfully established themselves as shadow leaders in Michigan Republican circles and big-money facilitators of the party's national ambitions, created successful models for others to emulate:

> Buoyed by the success in Michigan, the DeVoses have exported a scaled-down version of that template into other states, funding an archipelago of local political action committees and advocacy organizations to ease the proliferation of charter schools in Indiana, New Jersey, Ohio, Iowa, Virginia and Louisiana, among others. At the same time, DeVos-backed PACs have transformed the nature of American political campaigns. By showing the success of independent PACs that answered to a few deep-pocketed donors rather than a broad number of stakeholders associated with a union or chamber of commerce, for instance, the DeVoses precipitated the monsoon of independent expenditures that has rained down upon politicians for the past decade.

If you were to freeze-frame the story of the DeVos family right there, it would be an impressive enough story -- world-shaping wealth accumulated and distributed, a single-minded political vision channeled and disseminated. But now, we're getting to the good part -- where Betsy DeVos takes her turn at center stage.

Betsy DeVos began her career in the Michigan Republican Party in the early 1980s, moving her way up the ranks from precinct delegate to RNC state committeewoman. In 1996, Republican Governor John Engler

---

[16] Stanton, Z. (15 January 2017). How Betsy DeVos Used God and Amway to Take Over Michigan Politics. *Politico Magazine*. https://www.politico.com/magazine/story/2017/01/betsy-dick-devos-family-amway-michigan-politics-religion-214631

tapped her to be the chairwoman of the Michigan Republican Party, a move that would provide DeVos with the foundation to cement her dominance of the Republican landscape statewide.

The preceding circumstances of Engler's decision are worth noting. As Engler went into his 1994 campaign, seeking a second term in the statehouse, he was still trying to enact one of his signature campaign promises -- a 20 percent reduction in the state's property taxes. The matter had gotten bogged down in the legislature, with Democrats demanding that the revenue hole this tax reduction would create be filled by other means. The matter was at an impasse when then-state senator Jennifer Granholm, seeking to only comedically highlight her belief that Engler's proposal was fiscally irresponsible, proposed a stunt amendment that would eliminate the state's income tax entirely. Engler, unexpectedly, called her bluff. In a matter of hours, Michigan's state legislature got rid of property taxes, immediately defunding the public school system. During the ensuing budget scrum, Engler managed to give Betsy DeVos a great gift -- he legalized charter schools in Michigan.

When Engler placed DeVos at the head of the state party in the aftermath of this legislative melee, he imagined that he'd be getting a true partner -- someone with whom he could synchronize his vision. DeVos had other ideas, and after Engler won his third term, she would put them into action -- launching a campaign to legalize school vouchers across Michigan. Because the state constitution didn't allow public money to be shuttled to religious schools, DeVos had to change the constitution, and hatched a plan to get a constitutional amendment on the ballots by the 2000 election cycle.

But this move caught Engler off-guard. In his opinion, the time wasn't ripe to go all-in on such a proposal. He didn't feel that the public was behind the idea, nor did he believe they could be persuaded in time enough to win at the polls. His message was clear: he wouldn't back DeVos' play. Betsy, resolute as ever, resigned from the state party and went it alone -- into the teeth of fierce, and well-organized, opposition. By the time the votes were counted on Election Night, Engler looked like the prescient one -- nearly seven in ten voters opposed the amendment, and DeVos was taking heat for goosing Democratic turnout and sending Debbie Stabenow to the U.S. Senate to claim the seat of incumbent Republican Spencer Abraham.

DeVos' ambitious stunt had failed, leaving Republican blood on the street. But those who were inclined to believe that she had dealt herself a fatal self-own turned out to be tragically mistaken. As Zach Stanton recounted in Politico:

> There was a silver lining for the DeVoses, albeit one not immediately apparent. They had established a purity test for fellow Republicans: Had they supported Prop 1? And in unintentionally contributing to Senator Abraham's loss, they had created a scenario in which, once Engler was term-limited in January 2003, the state GOP would be without any marquee statewide officeholders. No governor. Neither U.S. senator. An attorney general and secretary of state without any previous statewide experience.
>
> There was a power vacuum in the Republican Party, and the DeVoses were the only ones who could fill it. Which they did, with lots and lots of money.

In 2001, the DeVoses bankrolled the foundation of the Great Lakes Education Project, which quickly came to be a preeminent force in Michigan politics. By the next election cycle, the money GLEP had in its coffers far exceeded what any Democratic-leaning organization of prominence could boast. What's more, GLEP's deep pockets proved to be more than sufficient to put the fear of God into Republicans who may have been disinclined to support Betsy DeVos' agenda with full throat. If you were a Republican state legislator with the inclination to slow-foot DeVos' vision to remake Michigan's school system, GLEP would unleash fury on the airwaves, and work to defeat you in your primary. The American Federation of Teachers, which had historically backed legislators in a bipartisan manner, quickly discovered that their endorsements and campaign donations were toxic to Republican state legislators. AFT was finding their checks returned.

It took time, but years of GLEP's pressure, influence, and tall dollars resulted in the outcome DeVos sought, a Michigan Republican Party that sung brightly from the DeVos family hymnal. And while Michigan voters rejected her husband Dick's charms in 2006, re-electing Democratic Governor Jennifer Granholm by a 56-42% margin in his effort to self-fund his own way to the statehouse, DeVos just kept building on the ashes of another temporary setback. By the time Granholm's term-limited time was up, the DeVos family had finally cemented their political dominance.

After the gubernatorial loss, Betsy encouraged her husband to found his own school that would put his love of private flying to good use, out of which West Michigan Aviation Academy was born.

"Sometime after that loss, Betsy challenged him to do something with his passion of aviation because he's a pilot," said Patrick Cwayna, the school's chief executive officer.

"She's the motivator behind him founding this school," he said. "But Dick is the upfront guy. Just because I know Dick and I know how they work as a couple, I know she's incredibly supportive, but he's the one who is engaged in the daily operations."

Michigan has now been remade according to DeVos' vision. There's no cap on the number of charter schools in Michigan, and they are the most lightly regulated charters in America. Eighty percent of those charters are run by for-profit entities -- again, the most of any state in the country.

Matthew Diemer, an associate professor in the University of Michigan's School of Education, says that it's "unfair and knee-jerk reactionary" to finger DeVos as "the cause of all the problems in Detroit and Michigan [schools]." "That's not true, and not fair," he says. Nevertheless, he notes that her political victories have had their share of deleterious effects statewide:

> Unfortunately, most of the evidence seems to suggest that charter schools do about the same, slightly worse, sometimes slightly better than traditional public schools, but they have this detrimental effect of taking money away from the public school system. And those parents and children, sometimes those parents pull children who are highly engaged away from the public school system and a charter. So it has the net effect of reducing the quality or funding for the public school system.

The Michigan Economic Center's Austin concurs:

> Most of the charters provide a worse level of education. We have 350 new school districts, which are charter schools and cyber schools, that have opened and they do market, you know, to vulnerable parents and say, Oh, here's a bright new shiny, you know, George Washington Carver Academy. And it's open as a storefront in Detroit or somewhere, it's safe and they do get

people to enroll. And the $7,000 with the kid follows that student, then if that school, of which we have too many, those kids don't get a very good education. They lose. And meanwhile, while you're taking 10, 20, 30 percent of the students out of the traditional public schools, who have, you know, 10, 20, 30 percent less revenue to pay teachers, to have counseling. And you have kids left in the traditional public schools that are more special needs, that are more expensive even, so it's a lose lose proposition. Everyone's getting a worse education.

Diemer observes that one of DeVos' larger aims seems to be directed at the "de-professionalization" of teachers. To Devos, teaching is "not a profession."

"It's something anybody can do, you know, just go to this program for a couple of weekends and we'll teach you a couple of techniques and you can be a teacher," says Diemer. "So there's this 'anybody can do it' mantra that underlies this move towards privatization," he explains. Moreover, for DeVos, Diemer says, the push for school vouchers and de-professionalizing teachers is "partly to have more religious schools" in the state. Indeed, while DeVos hasn't managed to fully breach the firewall between church and state in the way her failed amendment push would have succeeded in doing, the lack of regulatory oversight has allowed charter schools with a decidedly religious bent to slip into the system and siphon off a share of the taxpayer largesse.

DeVos has been at a loss to explain the abject failure of her vision in Michigan. So she has taken to waving away the very idea of statistics as a way to measure progress or setbacks.

"I hesitate to talk about all schools in general because schools are made up of individual students attending them," DeVos told Leslie Stahl when asked about the poor results in Michigan.

Okay, if data doesn't do it for you, how about anecdotes?

"Have you seen the really bad schools? Maybe try to figure out what they're doing?" Stahl asked.

"I have not intentionally visited schools that are underperforming," she said.

"Maybe you should," Stahl offered.

"Maybe I should. Yes," said Betsy DeVos, the secretary of education.

But the DeVossian vision hardly ends with remaking Michigan's education system. Ahead of the 2012 election, the DeVos family mobilized, creating a new "purity test" for Republicans -- unflagging support to transform Michigan, the state most commonly associated with labor union strength, into a right-to-work state. When Rick Snyder succeeded in winning back the statehouse for the GOP in the ensuing gubernatorial election, he did so with public reassurances to labor leaders in the state that such a move was off the table -- reassurances he repeated after Election Day.

But by the end of November, Michigan's airwaves were once again the venue for a blitz of DeVos-funded advertisements, promoting the right-to-work proposal, and once again the fear was felt. Snyder caved, and the right-to-work measure passed the state legislature. And in a bit of clever legislative skullduggery, the right-to-work bill that was enacted contained a small appropriation, which was noteworthy in only one way -- its inclusion precluded any possibility that the right-to-work bill could be reversed by public referendum.

As Politico's Stanton recounted:

> It isn't known what, if anything, the DeVoses said to Governor Snyder to change his mind and detonate this atomic bomb in Michigan politics. But Snyder would've been under no illusions about the possible consequences of inaction. "There was all kinds of scuttlebutt that if Snyder didn't sign up for right-to-work in 2012, he would've bought himself a primary in 2014," says Demas of Inside Michigan Politics. "I think Snyder understands the powerful place the DeVoses have in Michigan, and that it's often more trouble than it's worth to tangle with them."

Further legislation banned employers from processing union dues -- while leaving corporations with the right to deduct PAC money straight from paychecks. As former Michigan state representative Ellen Lipton told The Baffler's Jennifer Berkshire, "They won...it may have taken them longer than they wanted, but they won."

Indeed, Michigan's long war between labor and capital was over, and the DeVoses were victorious. And that victory earned would be a victory shared -- the DeVos blueprint proved to be easily exportable to other states, for other Republican-controlled legislatures to follow.

John Austin says that this was "exactly the point the DeVoses were going for." "The DeVos agenda," he says, is not really an "education agenda." Rather, it "has been largely a political agenda about destroying the Democratic Party and helping the Republican -- the extreme right wing Republicans -- win elections." He continues:

> They've been the Republican Party leaders in Michigan and funders and bankrollers of its right-wing agenda and a big part of that agenda, strategically has been, "How do we disadvantage Democrats and advantage the right wing Republicans? Oh, if we destroy the public school establishment and the unions, that will be helpful to our cause." So they fund the elections and insist on loyalty of the right wing Republican, which also lead to gerrymandering. They took over the legislature and gerrymandered even more on after 2010 to ensure that Democrats couldn't get elected to Congress or the state legislature. They spent their money and their efforts to expand [school] choice and allow anyone to open a charter school or cyber-school even if they don't educate kids. It is a purposeful strategy to create destabilizing markets where dollars and support for traditional public schools disappear. And it also has the effect of destroying learning outcomes for both kids and their parents."

"The traditional public schools are incredibly diminished and they can't win elections and the teachers unions can't make big contributions to Democratic candidates," he says. "And so it's been very successful."

The popular characterization of Betsy DeVos is that she's a bit of a bumbler, constantly out of her depths, more likely than not to make a dog's breakfast out of whatever task she has at hand. There are moments in her career that definitely fuel that meme. She's been at the center of some high-profile electoral failures. Her unregulated Michigan charter schools have largely done a dreadful job meeting minimum academic standards. She's had more than her share of public gaffes. And the fact that she has now ended up as a star in President Donald Trump's constellation of kakistocracy surely doesn't help -- though it's worth noting that she'd have almost assuredly ended up on the Cabinet shortlist of any of the Republicans who battled Trump in the 2016 Republican primary.

But those caught up in the happy notion that DeVos is an anthropomorphic failure factory really need to look again. The truth is, she's been a highly effective member of a vastly successful political dynasty, and for someone who married into the Amway family, she is nevertheless a pure product of the values that Amway has long espoused -- the ruthless organization, the intense religiosity, the ability to transform failure into a platform for greater successes, and the fierce devotion to long-term thinking and slow-and-steady strategy.

In short, she's no dummy. The empire she has had a solid hand in building is tangible, perhaps permanent. Much like Trump, she's underestimated, but her accomplishments exist. But it's important to note that she has a few important things that Trump lacks, chief among them being a set of well-hewn core political beliefs, a plan to act on them, and a record of getting them done. And while she'd stumble badly during her confirmation hearings, requiring the rescue of Mike Pence's tie-breaking vote -- she would very quickly, and very ruthlessly, get back down to the family business.

CHAPTER THREE: DILETTANTE

From the very moment Betsy DeVos' Senate confirmation hearing kicked off on January 17, 2017, there was an unmistakable sign that President Trump's newly anointed education czarina was in for a rough ride.

Republican operatives who had handled her confirmation training were watching nervously. Her lead sherpa through the process, Lauren Maddox, was a registered lobbyist with the Podesta Group -- not a former lobbyist now getting back into public service, but an actual, current lobbyist paid by corporate clients for her ability to sway public policy. Maddox, a former Bush administration Education Department official, as well as a past aide to House Speaker Newt Gingrich, had the task of educating DeVos on education.

DeVos made a less than ideal student. "Her mind didn't naturally go to different places," recalled one participant in the confirmation training sessions, rather charitably. "She was a very visual person, so she had to have the stuff color coded in front of her."

That, though, presented its own problems, as the team knew that if the color-coded flashcards were visible on camera, it would be a major embarrassment, so pains were made to keep them off screen. "You don't wanna have all those things out there because people can see it," the GOP official noted.

Fortunately, DeVos would get some help during her hearings from the person running the show. The Republican chairman of the Senate Committee on Health, Education, Labor, and Pensions (HELP), Lamar

Alexander -- himself a former U.S. Secretary of Education who'd served as the senior senator from Tennessee since 2003 -- gaveled the hearing into session and immediately started setting some rather unusual ground rules, proclaiming that each committee member would be granted only five minutes to question the nominee. Alexander asserted that this was to be the hearing's "Golden Rule" -- a precedent he claimed had been firmly established by past confirmation hearings including those of President Barack Obama's nominees for the Education Department.

It was not, as Democratic ranking member Patty Murray made clear, a precedent with which anyone on the committee had hitherto been familiar. And despite Alexander's repeated protests that it was, in fact, "as clear a precedent as I could think of," it led to every Democrat on the panel accusing Alexander of working to shield DeVos from their scrutiny.

Of course, Democrats' demand for additional questioning time was driven by another precedent: none of the previous nominees being held out by Alexander as examples were quite so burdened with ethical quandaries. Indeed, DeVos' hearing had, at this point, already been postponed due to her failure to complete her required review with the U.S. Office of Government Ethics, a failure which only primed the pump for increased suspicion and a wider inquiry. From her history of shady investments, dodgy campaign violations, and conflicts of interest in the education sphere, DeVos had enough ethical red flags to sell them at wholesale prices.

And beyond that, DeVos had, by this point, a long, well-documented history of antipathy toward America's public schools -- a veritable feast for anyone with the moxie to hold her to account.

So it's not hard to see why Democrats entered the hearing ready to dig down into DeVos' murky history and her ideological beliefs, or why Alexander would want to use the convenience of his HELP committee chairmanship to throw up as many procedural barricades as he could. The goal for Alexander was to shelter the billionaire heiress from tough questioning. The goal for DeVos was not to create any viral videos.

As it would turn out, however, Alexander's efforts proved insufficient. Really, nothing short of cancelling the hearing entirely would have helped DeVos avoid exposing the fact that for someone with such strongly held opinions about education, she knew precious little about education.

In fact, one of the most widely puzzled over answers that DeVos gave during her confirmation hearing was in response to a very direct question, posed by then-Minnesota Senator Al Franken. When Franken started in on his line of inquiry, he began by asking her a seemingly softball question regarding the appropriate way to use standardized tests. "I would like your views," he asked DeVos, "on the relative advantage of doing assessments and using them to measure proficiency, or to measure growth."

It was, without a doubt, a wonky question -- the sort that would likely not have been familiar to anyone outside of the education industry. But in terms of beginning a line of inquiry, this was a rather innocuous place to start. Growth versus proficiency is not considered an obscure education policy debate, but a rather fundamental one. Those who are concerned with "proficiency" favor measuring whether children are achieving certain education milestones in a timely fashion, like the ability to read at grade level. Those who take up the "growth" side of the debate would prefer that testing account for whether children are making sufficient progress over the course of a school year.

In other words, if a teacher lifts a student from a first grade to a fourth grade level in a single year, is that a success even if they are in sixth grade? How should the school be evaluated in such a case? As standardized testing has exploded across U.S public schools, how to properly interpret the results of the tests has grown increasingly important, and debated.

The "No Child Left Behind Act," signed into law by President George W. Bush, was instrumental in making measures of proficiency the gold standard in the testing-and-accountability regime that has enveloped K-12 education in recent years. Meanwhile, growth-standard advocates argue that schools should not be punished for low-achieving students as long as the children are making consistent, year-to-year gains.

As The Atlantic's Alia Wong noted at the time, it was a critical question to ask DeVos, because whatever side of that debate DeVos happened to support had wide-ranging ramifications for how she might govern at the Department of Education:

> The Every Student Succeeds Act[17] (ESSA), which replaced No Child Left Behind, generally allows states to come up with their own plans for how to hold schools accountable—whether it be through proficiency or growth or some combination of both. But

---

[17] U.S. Congress. S.1177-Every Student Succeeds Act. *Congress.gov.*
https://www.congress.gov/bill/114th-congress/senate-bill/1177/text

the law also requires that DeVos sign off[18] on their ESSA plans, most of which have yet to be finalized, but many of which are likely to have [sic] accountability proposals that resemble what they already have in place.[19] (That's largely because the vast majority of states have long had waivers[20] from the rigid No Child Left Behind law—tailored plans that in part allow them to shift away from proficiency and toward growth.)

In asking the question, Franken was simply trying to establish a benchmark with DeVos, a way to better assess her overall views on school accountability. He could not have possibly expected the answer he got.

"I think if I am understanding your question correctly around proficiency," said DeVos, "I would also correlate it to competency and mastery, so each student is measured according to the advancement they are making in each subject area."

"That's growth, that's not proficiency," interrupted Franken. "I'm talking about the debate between proficiency and growth, and what your thoughts are."

A gaffe in Washington is famously said to occur when a politician speaks the truth accidentally. This was a different sort of gaffe, an accidental revelation of a stunning level of ignorance. It turned out she had no thoughts on the question.

Elsewhere, at least, she had vague thoughts. When Senator Murray asked DeVos whether or not she would commit herself to neither working to privatize public schools, nor cutting "a single penny for public education," DeVos simply gave a boilerplate answer about how she looked forward to "working with you to talk about how to address the needs of all parents and students...to find common ground in ways we can solve those issues and empower parents to make choices on behalf of their children that are right for them."

"I take that as not being willing to commit to not privatize public schools," responded Murray.

---

[18] Klein, A. (28 November 2018). Final ESSA Accountability Rules Boost State Flexibility in Key Areas. *Education Week*. http://blogs.edweek.org/edweek/campaign-k-12/2016/11/ed_dept_releases_final_account.html

[19] Wong, A. (9 December 2015). The Bloated Rhetoric of No Child Left Behind's Demise. *The Atlantic*. https://www.theatlantic.com/education/archive/2015/12/the-bloated-rhetoric-of-no-child-left-behinds-demise/419688/

[20] (20 March 2013). NCLB Waivers: A State-by-State Breakdown. *Education Week*. https://www.edweek.org/ew/section/infographics/nclbwaivers.html

When it was Massachusetts Senator Elizabeth Warren's turn to question the nominee, Warren turned her attention to for-profit universities and the Education Department's role in policing such entities. Warren asked DeVos how she would go about protecting students from being scammed. When DeVos answered that she would be "vigilant," it wasn't enough for Warren, who wanted to know how, exactly, she'd set about ensuring that predatory fraudsters would not victimize students. DeVos did not seem to grasp that there were tools, like gainful employment regulations, already at her disposal to aid in this fight. And once DeVos was informed of her options, she refused to commit to using them, instead telling Warren that she would "review" those regulations.

"I don't understand about reviewing it," said a perplexed Warren. "We talked about this in my office. There are already rules in place to stop waste, fraud and abuse...Swindlers and crooks are out there doing back flips when they hear an answer like this."

And yes, there was that moment when DeVos, attempting to explain why it was sensible for "locales and states to decide" whether or not guns belong in public schools, cited the need for teachers to have "a gun in the school to protect from potential grizzlies." Never let it be said that DeVos couldn't serve up a much-needed viral headline to the media.

"The hearing is just a terrible place for her," the official who helped her prep concluded.

DeVos, reflecting later in her interview with 60 Minutes, concurred with that assessment. "I've not had a root canal, but I can imagine that a root canal might be more pleasant than that was," she guessed.

The word "incompetent" gets overused in Washington, but for many -- judging, perhaps, a little too prematurely -- it was a term that aptly described Betsy DeVos. Her confirmation hearing, it must be said, went a long way toward reinforcing that perception, revealing a nominee who often seemed as woefully adrift on the basics of education as she was certain that she knew the best possible way to oversee it.

And so, Congress' phone banks heaved and cracked under the volume of calls, beseeching her swift dismissal. Two Republican Senators, Alaska's Lisa Murkowski and Maine's Susan Collins, stunned at the opposition pouring through their phone lines, took heed and announced that they would be withholding their support for her nomination, while several others wavered.

Losing those two votes forced the Trump administration to hustle Vice President Mike Pence up to Capitol Hill to cast the tie-breaking vote on a Senate confirmation, something that had previously never been required. DeVos had made it, by the thinnest of margins -- the first Secretary of Education ever confirmed without bipartisan support. Pence would refer to casting the deciding vote -- a ritual humiliation for any administration -- as a "high honor."

But it was Collins and Murkowski who should be credited for doing the honorable thing -- looking past the ideological ambitions of their party in order to consider the needs of their own constituents. For both women, DeVos' devotion to charters and school vouchers posed a real threat, as their states feature far-flung communities for whom public school is the only available option. Choice is merely a word when there's only one school within miles and miles.

"I think that Mrs. DeVos has much to learn about our nation's public schools, how they work and the challenges they face," said Murkowski[21] in a speech on the Senate floor. "And I have serious concerns about a nominee to be Secretary of Education who has been so involved on one side of the equation, so immersed in the push for vouchers, that she may be unaware of what actually is successful within the public schools and also what is broken and how to fix them."

In this limited respect, Murkowski really had DeVos pegged. But even Murkowski failed to appreciate the extent of the nominee's inadequacies, because despite being "immersed in the push for vouchers," DeVos arrived in Washington with such a spotty record of both advocating for and implementing her grand designs, that even her fellow travelers in the voucher/charter movement -- a community of ersatz thought leaders who'd normally not think twice about redirecting public money to private-sector schemes or disemboweling a teachers' union -- were hesitant, if not wholly averse, to supporting her nomination.

For example, while New York Magazine politics writer Jonathan Chait -- who frequently bedevils liberals for his unalloyed support for charter schools -- didn't find DeVos to be Trump's most objectionable nominee, he nevertheless proclaimed his opposition to DeVos on the grounds that she was an incapable avatar of the charter school movement. "It's important to understand what is actually concerning about DeVos," Chait wrote. "In addition to lacking policy heft, she is in the grip of simplistic ideas about education and she sees parental choice

---

[21] Joseph, C. (1 February 2017). Trump's Secretary of Education pick Betsy DeVos in jeopardy as two Republicans announce opposition. *Daily News*. http://www.nydailynews.com/news/politics/gop-senators-vote-trump-pick-betsy-devos-article-1.2961587

as a panacea. If parents can choose which school to send their children to, she believes, competition will inevitably force improvement. From the standpoint of center-left education reforms, this is dangerously simplistic."

Chait, noting that charter school performance varies widely across the country, targeted Michigan's charter system -- which DeVos had a strong hand in shaping -- for its lack of sufficient oversight[22] and its utterly dismal nationwide ranking.[23]

Michigan State Board of Education President John Austin, who is also a strong supporter of charter schools, concurred, telling Politico: "The bottom line should be, 'Are kids achieving better or worse because of this expansion of choice?'" His state's policies, Austin said, were "destroying learning outcomes." "The DeVoses were a principal agent of that," he asserted.

It's easy to paint a fretful portrait of DeVos. Her track record as a reformer, coupled with her consistent inability to account for the most basic educational concepts, is enough to leave anyone with the firm impression that she simply does not know what she's doing.

But to borrow from Marco Rubio, a supporter of DeVos, "let's dispel once and for all with this fiction" that Betsy DeVos doesn't know what she's doing.

She knows exactly what she's doing.

---

[22] Harris, Douglas. (25 November 2016). Betsy DeVos and the Wrong Way to Fix Schools. *The New York Times*. https://www.nytimes.com/2016/11/25/opinion/betsy-devos-and-the-wrong-way-to-fix-schools.html

[23] Emma, C., Wermund, B., Hefling, K. (9 December 2016). DeVos' Michigan schools experiment gets poor grades. *Politico*. https://www.politico.com/story/2016/12/betsy-devos-michigan-school-experiment-232399

CHAPTER FOUR: SABOTEUR

With her well-documented background in mind, DeVos' critics were well within bounds to be on their guard as she assumed a role that would have the broad power to alleviate, or exacerbate, the burdens of vulnerable populations. And by the time she completed her first year at the Department of Education, their reservations would prove to be well-founded.

It wouldn't take long for DeVos to set the kind of tone that affirmed these misgivings. On February 27, after DeVos emerged from a "listening session" with the leaders of some of America's Historically Black Colleges and Universities (HBCUs), her office **put out a press release**[24] that set a new world record for tone-deafness.

"A key priority for this administration is to help develop opportunities for communities that are often the most underserved," the statement read. "Rather than focus solely on funding, we must be willing to make the tangible, structural reforms that will allow students to reach their full potential."

If only the statement had ended there, it would have been a nice little button on her meeting with HBCU stakeholders. Unfortunately, things went right off the rails.

---

[24] Department of Education Press Office. (28 February 2017). Statement from Secretary of Education Betsy DeVos Following Listening Session with Historically Black College and University Leaders. *U.S. Department of Education*. https://www.ed.gov/news/press-releases/statement-secretary-education-betsy-devos-following-listening-session-historically-black-college-and-university-leaders

Historically Black Colleges and Universities (HBCUs) have done this since their founding. They started from the fact that there were too many students in America who did not have equal access to education. They saw that the system wasn't working, that there was an absence of opportunity, so they took it upon themselves to provide the solution.

HBCUs are real pioneers when it comes to school choice. They are living proof that when more options are provided to students, they are afforded greater access and greater quality. Their success has shown that more options help students flourish.

Within the space of one hundred words, DeVos' Department of Education had heralded the discriminatory practices of the Jim Crow South as having paved the way for her pet project, school choice, as if black students living under segregation had any other educational options open to them.

In practice things often went poorly when southern blacks attempted to gain admission to the same educational institutions their white peers attended. When James Meredith, the first black student admitted to the University of Mississippi, attempted to go to class in 1962, he had to be accompanied[25] by national guardsmen after a violent campus riot claimed two lives. An unyielding Mississippi Governor Ross Barnett had boldly declared that he was "a Mississippi segregationist...and proud of it," and urged white Mississippians to "respond" in a call to arms against Meredith, who he depicted as an invader.

There really wasn't much choice available to black students, even as recently as the latter half of the 20th century. And HBCUs were surely not established as a way to increase competition in the educational marketplace.

Reactions to DeVos' statement were harsh and swift.[26] Senator Chris Murphy, a Democrat from Connecticut, called the statement "BANANAS" on Twitter. His colleague, Senator Claire McCaskill from Missouri, piled

[25] Elliott, D. (1 October 2012). Integrating Ole Miss: A Transformative Deadly Riot. *NPR.* https://www.npr.org/2012/10/01/161573289/integrating-ole-miss-a-transformative-deadly-riot

[26] MacNeal, C. (28 February 2017). DeVos Slammed For Calling Colleges 'Pioneers' Of School Choice. *Talking Points Memo.* https://talkingpointsmemo.com/livewire/devos-slammed-for-linking-black-colleges-school-choice

on, tweeting, "Totally nuts. DeVos pretending that establishment of historically black colleges was about choice not racism." DeVos spent the following afternoon on Twitter herself, backpedaling her previous statement.[27]

No amount of backpedaling could earn DeVos forgiveness, however. In May, when DeVos appeared as the commencement speaker at Daytona Beach, Florida's HBCU Bethune-Cookman, students booed and turned their backs on her.[28] While much ink has been spilled over the alleged illiberalism on college campuses -- and for the school's part, Bethune-Cookman president Edison O. Jackson did chastise the hecklers for their behavior -- it's hard to blame Bethune-Cookman's graduates. DeVos had, after all, slandered the origin story of the very sort of college from which they had matriculated -- and erased the long historical struggle that got them to that point.

But beyond the reaction of Bethune-Cookman's graduates, DeVos' gaffe -- if that's what it was -- sent a signal that she might not have the best interests of marginalized groups at heart. She seemed comfortable co-opting whatever she could find to advance her own political agenda. In fact, it was that agenda that likely led Bethune-Cookman to invite DeVos to its commencement ceremony in the first place: the HBCU had recently entered into an affiliate agreement with the Arizona Summit Law School, under which they'd be encouraging Bethune-Cookman graduates to attend the for-profit college as a part of a scholarship program in an arrangement that the Intercept's Zaid Jilani reported[29] was "a prelude to a possible acquisition."

As Jilani discovered, Arizona Summit was rife with problems, with only a quarter of its graduates succeeding in passing the Arizona bar exam on their first attempt. In a New York Times op-ed titled, "How To Con Black Law Students: A Case Study,"[30] Above The Law editor Elie Mystal savaged Bethune-Cookman's arrangement with Arizona Summit, writing:

[27] Alcindor, Y. (28 February 2017). After Backlash, DeVos Backpedals on Remarks on Historically Black Colleges. *The New York Times.* https://www.nytimes.com/2017/02/28/us/politics/betsy-devos-historically-black-colleges-statement.html?_r=0

[28] Green, E. (10 May 2017). Bethune-Cookman Greets Betsy DeVos With Turned Backs. *The New York Times.* https://www.nytimes.com/2017/05/10/us/politics/betsy-devos-bethune-cookman-commencement.html?_r=0

[29] Jilani, Z. (29 May 2017). Bethune Cookman Had A Reason To Invite Betsy DeVos To Give That Calamitous Commencement Speech. *The Intercept.*
https://theintercept.com/2017/05/29/bethune-cookman-actually-had-a-reason-to-invite-betsy-devos-to-give-that-calamatous-commencement-speech/

[30] Mystal, E. (20 March 2017). How to Con Black Law Students: A Case Study. *The New York Times.* *https://www.nytimes.com/2017/03/20/opinion/how-to-con-black-law-students-a-case-study.html*

But encouraging African-American students to attend Arizona Summit will not help them achieve their goals. It will hobble them. Going to a law school that doesn't prepare most of its students to pass the bar is not an "opportunity," unless "opportunity" means being saddled with debt that you'll spend the rest of your life trying to pay back.

"For-profit schools like Arizona Summit," wrote Mystal, "prey on students with high aspirations but little knowledge about how the postgraduate system really works." And the person who would be ensuring that Arizona Summit would be held accountable -- and potentially blowing up Bethune-Cookman's profitable arrangements -- was honored guest DeVos.

But if Bethune-Cookman's graduates were primarily concerned about DeVos' antipathy for the civil rights movement, it would soon prove to be a warranted fear. In June, ProPublica's Jessica Huseman and Annie Waldman reported[31] that the Trump administration was "quietly [rolling] back civil rights efforts" across the federal government. In their report, DeVos' Department of Education took the "let's hit civil rights protections" version of a star turn.

In a June 8 internal memo sent to Department of Education staff, acting assistant secretary for civil rights Candice Jackson "laid out plans to loosen requirements into civil rights complaints."[32] As Huseman and Waldman reported, the Obama administration had opted to take a more aggressive approach to investigating civil rights complaints. Under their directives, "individual complaints related to complex issues such as school discipline, sexual violence and harassment, equal access to educational resources, or racism at a single school might have prompted broader probes to determine whether the allegations were part of a pattern of discrimination or harassment." To that end, civil rights investigators were directed to obtain "three years of complaint data" to determine whether or not structural institutional problems needed to be addressed to remedy the situation beyond the individual complaint.

---

[31] Huseman, J., Waldman, A. (6 June 2017). Trump Administration Quietly Rolls Back Civil Rights Efforts Across Federal Government. *ProPublica*. https://www.propublica.org/article/trump-administration-rolls-back-civil-rights-efforts-federal-government
[32] Waldman, A. OCR Instructions to the Field re Scope of Complaints. *ProPublica*. https://www.documentcloud.org/documents/3863019-doc0074242017060911824.html

Critics of this approach maintain that such broad investigations impose too many costs and demands on schools. But civil rights leaders insist that abandoning the Obama-era framework for something narrower would only help schools sweep their systemic problems under the rug.

Catherine Lhamon, who led the Education Department's Office for Civil Rights (OCR) from August 2013 until January 2017 and currently chairs the United States Commission on Civil Rights, called the narrowing of OCR's investigations "stunning" and "dangerous."[33] Taking an expansive view of the potential for harm is important, she explained, "because if you look only at the most recent year, you won't necessarily see the pattern."

Much like DeVos, Jackson had a past that made casting a critical eye on her civil rights decisions a mandatory exercise. As Waldman reported elsewhere[34], while Jackson was an undergraduate at Stanford, she "gravitated" toward a section of her calculus class that "provided students with extra help," only to discover that this remedial section was set up to aid minority students. She took to the pages of the Stanford Review to complain, writing, "I am especially disappointed that the University encourages these and other discriminatory programs...We need to allow each person to define his or her own achievements instead of assuming competence or incompetence based on race."

Elsewhere, Jackson contended that "No one, least of all the minority student, is well served by receiving special treatment based on race or ethnicity." Additionally, Jackson's past writings included praise[35] for libertarian economist Murray Rothbard, and his opposition to the Civil Rights Act of 1964. None of this seemed particularly promising for an office whose mission involves specifically protecting students from discrimination.

In addition to Jackson's proposed rollbacks of Obama-era protections, DeVos also had, by this time, proposed stripping the Office for Civil Rights of 40 positions, which would add further limitations to its

---

[33] U.S. Commission on Civil Rights. Biography of Catherine E. Lhamon (Chair). http://www.usccr.gov/about/bio/Lhamon.php

[34] Waldman, A. (14 April 2017). DeVos Pick to Head Civil Rights Office Once Said She Faced Discrimination for Being White. *ProPublica*. https://www.propublica.org/article/devos-candice-jackson-civil-rights-office-education-department

[35] Jackson, C. Rothbard's The Ethics of Liberty: What It Is and What It Is Not. *Ludwig von Mises Institute*. https://web.archive.org/web/20130120205354/http:/www.mises.org/journals/scholar/Jackson1.PDF

ability to conduct investigations. On June 27, thirty Democratic senators put their objections -- ranging from the gutting of staff to her unwillingness to "take actions to protect transgender students" -- on the record in a letter. "You claim to support civil rights and oppose discrimination," they wrote,[36] "but your actions belie your assurances."

DeVos' inability to properly marry her actions and her assurances would crop up again in early September, when she announced that she would be rescinding another Obama-era directive, intended to provide greater protections to victims of campus sexual assault under Title IX. In a speech at George Mason University, DeVos complained that the "system established by the prior administration has failed too many students," and that "survivors, victims of a lack of due process and campus administrators have all told me that the current approach does a disservice to everyone involved."

DeVos did, at least, have a leg to stand on. Specifically, in 2011, the Department of Education's Office for Civil Rights issued a "Dear Colleague" letter that stipulated that universities had to apply a "preponderance of the evidence" standard to sexual assault cases, replacing the previous "beyond a shadow of doubt" standard. As Slate's Mark Joseph Stern reported at the time[37], this meant that anyone accused of sexual assault "must be disciplined if a fact-finder is 51 percent certain [they are] guilty." The same letter also discouraged the practice of allowing the accused to cross-examine their accuser on the grounds that victims could find it "traumatic or intimidating," and permitted schools to "forbid the accused from using a lawyer throughout the Title IX process."

Law professor Lara Bazelon, writing in Politico, agreed that these Obama-era guidelines had "created a new class of victims: students expelled and branded sexual assailants based on a disciplinary process that deprived them of crucial rights," and recommended that the standard for proof be raised from "preponderance of the evidence" to "clear and convincing evidence," as well as restoring due process rights to the accused.

"As someone who's studied and reported in-depth on this complex, emotionally fraught issue, I've come to the conclusion that the Obama-

---

[36] Letter to Betsy DeVos from U.S. Senators. (27 June 2017). *United States Senate.*
https://www.documentcloud.org/documents/3878600-Senators-Letter-Betsy-DeVos-ED-OCR.html
[37] Stern, M. (11 September 2017). One Cheer for DeVos. *Slate.*
http://www.slate.com/articles/news_and_politics/jurisprudence/2017/09/betsy_devos_is_right_t hat_colleges_trample_on_the_rights_of_accused_sexual.html

era guidelines got the policy wrong," wrote Bazelon. "And before we condemn the education secretary, let's give her a chance to get it right."

Nevertheless, there was a substantial debate in the legal community over whether the Obama-era policy was worthy of scuppering. And many experts noticed big gaps in DeVos' understanding of the underlying issues.

In an interview with Jezebel's Prachi Gupta[38], Jess Davidson, the managing director of End Rape on Campus, found it troubling that DeVos equated the trauma of sexual assault with that of a wrongful accusation: "She really does not understand the survivor's experience, the neurobiology of trauma, and its lasting impact on students, and that's a problem because students that are experiencing that lifelong impact of trauma and are trying to have equal access to their education afterward, they really need government officials who understand the impact in order to help them get the accommodations that give them equal access to education."

The National Women's Law Center's Alexandra Brodsky told Gupta that DeVos had demonstrated that she had no firm understanding of Title IX's regulatory environment. "She listed examples of schools making grave procedural errors as though they were the result of the guidance, instead of directly contrary to the guidance," said Brodsky, adding, "she seems to be attributing places where schools are breaking the law to the law—even though the obvious answer is to enforce the law."

All things being equal, it would not be unreasonable to expect the Obama administration's successor at the Department of Education to unwind these regulations, and it certainly would be a laudatory accomplishment to arrive at a middle ground that could be deemed just and equitable, with the ultimate goal of shrinking the number of people sexually assaulted on campus. But the atmosphere of misgivings that follows DeVos permeated the atmosphere. Mark Joseph Stern -- who began his Slate piece declaring that DeVos was "not particularly qualified to perform any aspect of her job" -- insisted that there was "good reason" to doubt her, noting that she had met[39] with "men's rights activists" who "dismiss claims of sexual abuse" out of hand, and that acting OCR head

---

[38] Cills, H. (5 December 2017). Students Accused of Sexual Misconduct Are Increasingly Filing Defamation Suits Against Their Accusers. *Jezebel.* https://jezebel.com/students-accused-of-sexual-misconduct-are-increasingly-1821026491

[39] Quinlan, C. (11 July 2017) Betsy DeVos meets with 'men's rights' activists. *Think Progress.* https://thinkprogress.org/devos-sexual-assault-bf7801b8264c/

Candice Jackson had claimed[40] "that '90 percent' of campus rape accusations 'fall into the category of 'we were both drunk' and 'she just decided that our last sleeping together was not quite right.'"

And as Bazelon pointed out, there was another thorny matter: "Because DeVos is a member of the Trump administration—and therefore, a surrogate for the man who famously bragged about sexually assaulting women— it's easy to focus on the messenger and dismiss the message."

DeVos' next move to undo protections for students who have long depended on the Department of Education for support was even less defensible than her Title IX decision. In October the Education Department sent out a newsletter casually announcing that it had rescinded 72 special education guidance documents that pertained to the rights of students with disabilities. The ED offered little explanation beyond stating that the documents were "outdated, unnecessary, or ineffective."

A few days later, outraged advocates realized the Department had quietly removed the documents over two weeks earlier and never told anyone.

Democratic leaders denounced the move. Representative Bobby Scott, from Virginia, witheringly referred to DeVos' decision as "the latest in a series of disturbing actions taken by the Trump administration to undermine civil rights for vulnerable Americans." Senator Kamala Harris of California tweeted that the Trump administration's "campaign against students with disabilities continues. We should be doing more, not less, to help them."

Though experts say that the decision to rescind those special education documents does not, for now, appear to be specifically harmful to students, the fact that federal officials seemed to regard such sensitive policymaking as a blasé exercise that didn't need to involve critical stakeholders raised many alarming red flags.

Denise Marshall, the executive director of the Council of Parent Attorneys and Advocates — a national group that protects the legal and civil rights of students with disabilities — told The Intercept that the ED's secretive behavior contributed to real chaos for many families. "We continue to lack any real information from the department on next steps,

---

[40] Green, E. Stolberg, S. (12 July 2017). Campus Rape Policies Get a New Look as the Accused Get DeVos's Ear. *The New York Times.* https://www.nytimes.com/2017/07/12/us/politics/campus-rape-betsy-devos-title-iv-education-trump-candice-jackson.html

so it's premature to know what the full impact will be or if substantive feedback provided by stakeholders will be considered," she said. "Suffice it to say, we remain very concerned."

Perhaps no one had a more succinct take on the consequences than Vilissa Thompson-- a South Carolina-based social worker and disability consultant -- who told Rewire, "It feels like the clock is being rolled back due to the attacks on the rights and policies that have been won over the past decades...It is disheartening that we have to take a stand on the basics: education, health care, et cetera. Instead of doing what it needed to fix gaps, the current administration is doing what it can to widen them."

Special education advocates have long feared how DeVos might treat students with disabilities given her steadfast, fundamentalist belief in school choice. How might the ideological billionaire think about expanding her school choice vision on a national scale while enforcing federal student protections under the Individuals with Disabilities Education Act? DeVos regularly suggests that everything is best left to the states and to parents, even though civil rights advocates know that the federal government has always been the linchpin mechanism for protecting marginalized groups.

Indeed during her confirmation hearing, DeVos seemed to not be terribly familiar with IDEA, and struggled mightily to answer even basic questions about it. When Senator Tim Kaine, a Democrat from Virginia, asked DeVos whether she believed that charter and private schools that receive federal funding should all be subject to IDEA, which requires public schools to guarantee the provision of a "free, appropriate public education" to students with disabilities, DeVos declared that it was a "matter...best left to the states." Repeated questioning from Kaine only pushed DeVos further and further astray, until he was finally compelled to ask DeVos, simply, if she agreed with the notion that "all schools that receive federal funding — public, public charter, private — should be required to meet [IDEA's] conditions." "I think that is certainly worth discussion," said DeVos, apparently unaware that she was, in that moment, amid this very discussion.

That discussion then included this surreal exchange:

> Kaine: If confirmed will you insist upon equal accountability in any K-12 school or educational program that receives taxpayer funding whether public, public charter or private?

DeVos: I support accountability.

Kaine: Equal accountability?

DeVos: I support accountability.

Kaine: Is that a yes or a no?

DeVos: I support accountability.

Kaine: Do you not want to answer my question?

DeVos: I support accountability.

Kaine: Let me ask you this. I think all schools that receive taxpayer funding should be equally accountable. Do you agree?

DeVos: Well they don't, they are not today.

Kaine: Well, I think they should. Do you agree with me?

DeVos: Well no--

Kaine: You don't agree with me.

Given that DeVos' own previous adventures in erecting a school choice regime featured an accountability standard so low that education outcomes suffered as a result, this was a fearful matter for special education advocates, who had no way of knowing whether DeVos might allow her pet charter schools to skate on IDEA's federal requirements. Though it's not uncommon for schools to violate the federal law, the point of IDEA is that it provides a way for parents and advocates to hold public schools accountable. But that accountability only works if the federal government is committed to IDEA enforcement — something DeVos seems reluctant to promise. Advocates also worry that many parents who enroll their children in private schools with publicly-funded vouchers might not be fully aware that they could be sacrificing federal

IDEA protections as a result. Would DeVos, an ardent voucher advocate, be willing to educate parents about the risks and tradeoffs of her beloved policy?

Later in DeVos' confirmation hearing, Senator Maggie Hassan, a Democrat from New Hampshire who has a son with cerebral palsy, affirmed that IDEA is a federal statute. "So do you stand by your statement a few minutes ago that it should be up to the states whether to follow it?" she asked the nominee.

"I may have confused it," DeVos bafflingly replied.

Special education advocates were already wary of the influence that former Alabama senator-turned-Trump Attorney General Jeff Sessions might have over the federal law that protected these students. In a 2000 speech on the Senate floor, Sessions had blasted IDEA as something that allowed "special treatment for certain children," and abetted the "decline in civility and discipline in classrooms across America."

Keep in mind, we are talking about students -- at all levels of primary and secondary education -- who face health challenges ranging from physical disabilities to chronic developmental conditions like Down's Syndrome and autism. Most of these students will struggle educationally throughout their lives, many won't ever perform adequately on standardized tests or keep up with their peers, and some won't ever go on to have normal lives and careers. But access to a quality education is one of the few things we as a country have guaranteed them: a legislative commitment that might both alleviate the massive burdens faced by parents raising disabled children, and an opportunity to provide these students with a real shot at a meaningful life. For parents and students facing such extraordinary challenges, IDEA really is a vital lifeline.

Some observers have looked at the Education Department's recent actions and identified even more fearful symmetry — particularly in the confluence of weakening Title IX protections and the seemingly inadequate commitment to protecting students with disabilities.

As Robyn Powell — a disability rights attorney — pointed out[41], people with disabilities are sexually assaulted at extremely high rates, "with some studies estimating that as many as 80 percent of people with

---

[41] Powell, R. (24 October 2017). How Betsy DeVos' Title IX Actions Will Hurt Students With Disabilities. *Rewire. https://rewire.news/article/2017/10/24/betsy-devos-title-ix-actions-will-hurt-students-disabilities/*

disabilities[42] have been sexually assaulted more than once." Another study conducted by the Department of Justice found that "people with disabilities are more than three times as likely to be sexually assaulted[43] than non-disabled people." Students with disabilities also face daunting challenges when they choose to disclose their abuse and seek justice against their abusers, ranging from police and campus officials who lack disability training, insufficient accessibility for those who use wheelchairs, and a lack of access to sign language interpreters.

Once they find themselves knit up in the criminal justice system, students with disabilities face daunting obstacles that others don't. And when the system can't properly assist them in surmounting these obstacles, the results can be dire. In one noteworthy case from 2014[44], a Georgia appeals court judge overturned the verdict of a jury that had found a man guilty of three counts of rape. The judge ordered a new trial on the grounds that the jury's decision was "strongly against the weight of the evidence." To the judge, the woman allegedly raped "didn't act like a victim and the man didn't act like a rapist." The reason he thought this? The woman in question had Down's Syndrome, and the judge felt her behavior didn't comport with that of typical victims.

In 2012, the Connecticut State Supreme Court made a similarly specious decision[45], overturning the sexual assault conviction of a man who'd forced himself on a woman with severe cerebral palsy. As Think Progress reported at the time, the Court reasoned that "the defendant could not be convicted if there was any chance that the victim could have communicated her lack of consent," and "since the victim in this case was capable of 'biting, kicking, scratching, screeching, groaning or gesturing," the Court ruled[46] that the victim could have communicated lack of consent in spite of her disability.

[42] National Statistics. *Rape Response Services*. http://www.rrsonline.org/?page_id=944

[43] Harrell, E. (July 2017). Crime Against Persons with Disabilities, 2009-2015 – Statistical Tables. *U.S. Department of Justice*. https://www.bjs.gov/content/pub/pdf/capd0915st.pdf

[44] Perry, D. (5 May 2014). Rape Cases: When judges just don't get it. *CNN*. http://www.cnn.com/2014/03/11/opinion/perry-rape-disabled-georgia/index.html

[45] Beauchamp, Z. (3 October 2012). Court Requires Disabled Rape Victim To Prove She Resisted, Calls for Evidence of 'Biting, Kicking, Scratching'. *Think Progress*. https://thinkprogress.org/court-requires-disabled-rape-victim-to-prove-she-resisted-calls-for-evidence-of-biting-kicking-814dcfd2cbc7/

[46] Rogers, C.J. Norcott, Palmer, Zarell, McLachlan, Eveleigh, and Harper. (17 October 2011). State of Connecticut v. Richard Fourtin. *Connecticut Law Journal*. http://www.jud.ct.gov/external/supapp/Cases/AROcr/CR307/307CR83.pdf

Powell, the disability rights attorney, noted that people with disabilities are already far less likely to report sexual abuse[47], not to mention that those who do come forward regularly encounter other barriers — such as inaccessible services. "The estimated 11 percent of U.S. college students[48] with disabilities will almost certainly be disproportionately affected by DeVos' actions," she concluded.

Soraya Chemaly, the director of the Women's Media Center Speech Project underscored[49] these risks. "Protections for students with disabilities and for victims of sexual assault were developed over years and by experts, for a reason," she said, adding that DeVos' decisions "will almost inevitably hurt the people most targeted and least likely to be able to advocate for themselves."

In effect, a pattern emerges: Betsy DeVos lends her support to policies that experts insist will harm the marginalized, all the while creating new opportunities for the worst actors to con, coerce, and cheat. Never mind that the government had built a regulatory system designed to protect vulnerable groups. As a dutiful member of the Trump administration, these protections are ripe for dismantlement, and the public funding that enabled legislative enforcement heads back into the pocketbooks of the nation's wealthiest Americans.

But while DeVos and her allies back ideas that threaten the livelihood of vulnerable students -- including ethnic minorities, transgender people, the disabled, and victims of sexual assault -- they are not, by any means, the only ones at risk.

---

[47] Davis, L. (August 2009). People with Intellectual Disability and Sexual Violence. *The Arc.* *https://www.thearc.org/what-we-do/resources/fact-sheets/sexual-violence*
[48] Martin, R. (30 October 2012). ABCs of Accommodations. *The New York Times.* http://www.nytimes.com/2012/11/04/education/edlife/guide-to-accommodations-for-college-students-with-disabilities.html?_r=0
[49] Perry, D. (24 October 2017). Assessing Betsy DeVos' Rollback on Disability Rights. *Pacific Standard.* https://psmag.com/education/betsy-devos-rolls-back-disability-rights

CHAPTER FIVE: PLUTOCRAT

Another important group of vulnerable students in America are those who find themselves deeply indebted, yet graduating into an economy still shaking off the after-effects of the 2008 financial crisis -- which took its toll on job opportunities across the nation, severely limiting the options for those who'd played by the rules, gotten their degrees, and now wanted to join the workforce.

It didn't take long for the new secretary to start mucking about with what thin protections these indebted students had available to them. On April 11, DeVos formally withdrew two memos issued by the Obama administration that offered guidance to the Federal Student Aid office -- responsible for servicing over $1 billion in student loans -- on how to provide better service to borrowers who wanted to manage, or even discharge, their student debt. For the Obama administration it was a late-in-arriving but vital course correction for the agency, which had hitherto acted mainly in the interest of maximizing repayment proceeds.

The Obama administration rightly faced tremendous pressure to tame the unruly world of student loan servicing, and make things fairer and more equitable for borrowers. Notably, there was a great need to get the Department of Education more fully involved in protecting consumers. As The Nation's David Dayen reported, the Department's "own inspector general found in 2014 that the department didn't even track borrower complaints, let alone engage in actual oversight."[50]

---

[50] U.S. Government Accountability Office. (17 September 2015). Education Could Do More to Help Ensure Borrowers Are Aware of Repayment and Forgiveness Options.

Much of the work being done to assist borrowers was conducted by the Consumer Financial Protection Bureau and the Government Accountability Office, which found the world of student loan servicing to be an Augean Stable[51] of cheats and mismanagement. As the Washington Post's Danielle Douglas-Gabriel reported[52] in April of 2017, the CFPB had documented numerous "instances of servicing companies providing inconsistent information, misplacing paperwork, or charging unexpected fees." And GAO researchers found that 70 percent of borrowers who had ended up in default would have qualified for lower monthly payment options that would have kept them in good graces -- had loan servicers bothered to provide them with the necessary information.

One of the Obama administration's critical aims was to curtail the likelihood that loan servicer contracts would be doled out to companies with past histories of harming or scamming debtors. Like so many federal memoranda, the orders issued by then-Education Secretary John King, stated these goals in very anodyne terms, such as "simplifying the repayment process" and "facilitating our oversight of servicing contractors." But to contractors, these words spoke volumes about a new demand for better customer service across the board. It was clear companies would need to provide more effective counseling for individual borrowers, to better inform them about what options they had in reducing payments.

Like other Obama-era guidelines the Education Department has rescinded, DeVos and her flacks didn't feel it necessary to justify their behavior in detail to the public. Indeed, in this case they cited only unspecific criticisms that the Obama administration's approach was "vague and full of shortcomings." Over time, however, DeVos would offer a somewhat more concrete vision of the future of loan servicing: one in which the nine-contractor field of firms that collectively serviced the universe of student loan borrowers would be reduced to a single-servicer, creating what Vice News' Peter A. McKay characterized as a "$1 trillion monopoly."[53] This prospect sent a shockwave of fear through student

---

https://www.gao.gov/products/GAO-15-663

[51] Perseus Project, Classics Department, Tufts University. The Augean Stables Hercules Cleans Up. http://www.perseus.tufts.edu/Herakles/stables.html

[52] Douglas-Gabriel, D. (11 April 2017). DeVos dials back consumer protections for student loan borrowers. *The Washington Post*. https://www.washingtonpost.com/news/grade-point/wp/2017/04/11/devos-dials-back-consumer-protections-for-student-loan-borrowers/?utm_term=.752c84f582cc

[53] McKay, P. (28 May 2017). Betsy DeVos will let one company handle all federal student loans. *VICE NEWS*. https://news.vice.com/en_us/article/9kdvw8/betsy-devos-will-let-one-company-handle-all-

loan reformers. As one student debt activist put it, "We've already seen a real lack of accountability among the servicers in helping people manage their repayments, which should be the real priority. Now that accountability issue is exploding because we're taking away what little competition there was in this area."

Given that Washington boasts a notorious contracting process — typically a low-ball bid, race to the bottom — better service from student loan contractors was going to necessarily involve the government paying them more money for the privilege of doing their job competently. DeVos, citing a Trump administration mandate to cut costs across the board, framed the decision to scuttle the Obama-era guidelines as a boon to taxpayers.

Nevertheless, you get what you pay for. And in practice, paying for loan service on the cheap opened the door to some appalling practices that should set any decent person's hair on fire. On a regular basis, servicers aimed to cart off as much cash as they possibly could, systematically duping borrowers by literally hiding cheaper options[54] from consumers and pushing them into repayment plans that increase their risk of default.[55] In other words, companies essentially pushed the risk that defaulting borrowers posed onto taxpayers, while simultaneously selling them on the notion that the low cost of their poor service was a virtue. One particularly egregious target of these schemes were active-duty members of the military.[56] In rescinding these Obama-era guidelines, DeVos has courted a return to this shoddy, sordid way of doing business.

What's more, her move created the possibility that some of the worst actors in the student loan servicing business would get renewed opportunities to hurt borrowers. One such firm was Navient Corp., a company that emerged as one of three finalists for the newest round of loan-servicing contracts, due to be signed in 2019. Navient, which had split off from Sallie Mae at a time when the loan servicing giant was facing

federal-student-loans

[54] Nasiripour, S., Resmovits, J. (3 September 2013). Sallie Mae Lags In Student Debt Relief Amid Ongoing Federal Probes. *Huffington Post*. https://www.huffingtonpost.com/2013/09/03/sallie-mae-student-debt_n_3839243.html

[55] Nasiripour, S. (25 February 2014). Elizabeth Warren: Sallie Mae May Be Hurting Borrowers, Taxpayers. *Huffington Post*. https://www.huffingtonpost.com/2014/02/25/elizabeth-warren-sallie-mae_n_4856200.html

[56] Nasiripour, S. (16 April 2014). Sallie Mae Cheated Soldiers On Federal Student Loans, Government Investigators Find. *Huffington Post*. https://www.huffingtonpost.com/2014/04/16/sallie-mae-servicemembers_n_5162736.html

probes from three different federal agencies and a half-dozen states into their business practices, had managed to almost immediately run afoul of the Consumer Financial Protection Bureau for, "systematically and illegally failing borrowers at every stage of repayment."

By the end of the Obama administration, the CFPB had emerged as one of the more dogged cops on the student loan beat. Their efforts were bolstered by an information-sharing arrangement with the Department of Education, which the CFPB used to research and rein in loan-servicer scofflaws.

In May of 2015, the CFPB launched a public inquiry into how to improve servicer practices, soliciting over 30,000 public comments. This set the stage for a report issued a few months later in which the federal agency expressed concern about the "sloppy, patchwork practices" that had created "widespread servicing failures." The CFPB pledged to establish a new roadmap for student loan servicing, including "clear and consistent industry-wide standards."

Among the CFPB's goals were holding servicers accountable by enforcing federal and state consumer protection laws, higher education laws, and federal servicing contracts with the Department of Education.

And so it came to pass that just days before Trump's inauguration, the CFPB announced it was filing suit against Navient, joining extant suits against the company that had previously been filed by attorneys general in Washington and Illinois. In their complaint, the CFPB accused the company of years of wrongdoing, including creating "obstacles to repayment by providing bad information, processing payments incorrectly, and failing to act when borrowers complained." The CFPB also alleged that Navient cheated debtors "out of their rights to lower repayments" -- meaning borrowers were forced to pay much more than they should have.

Naturally, Navient's CEO, Jack Remondi, reacted with strenuous objections. In an interview with the Washington Post, he accused the CFPB of being "far more interested in solutions through enforcement actions and legal suits" than in actually working hand-in-hand to fix the process. "We had been working with the regulators, particularly the CFPB since their inception, to find ways to improve the student loan program," Remondi insisted.

It is, however, an open question as to whether Remondi really wanted to see the types of improvement that would benefit borrowers at the expense of Navient's bottom line. In their March 24 motion to dismiss the CFPB's lawsuit, the company's lawyers did that thing where they said out loud something that had previously only been whispered: "There is no expectation that the servicer will act in the interest of the consumer."

As Bloomberg's Shahien Nasiripour reported[57], there was no small amount of shock over this colossal admission:

> "It's rare for a company to be this bold," said Jenny Lee, a former CFPB attorney now with the law firm Dorsey & Whitney LLP in Washington. "It's a sound legal argument, but it may not be the best public relations argument."

> Suzanne Martindale, a San Francisco-based attorney for Consumers Union, the advocacy arm of Consumer Reports, said Navient's claim raises questions as to whether borrowers are afforded their right to apply for income-based repayment plans. [David] Bergeron, [a] former Education Department official, and Rohit Chopra, formerly a student loan regulator with the CFPB, added that they couldn't recall ever hearing—in public or private—a loan servicer arguing that it wasn't required to counsel borrowers about their options.

Nevertheless, this court filing made it abundantly clear that Navient believed it to be eminently reasonable to actively obstruct their customers from availing themselves of cost-saving repayment options. "What this means for the Education Department is that it needs to fire Navient, damn the costs," argued Bergeron.

And it certainly wasn't the sort of declaration that would encourage dedicated public servants at the CFPB to abandon their regulatory efforts. However, it was apparently music to DeVos' ears. The Education Secretary has proven to be a determined opponent to both bringing Navient to heel, as well as to increasing oversight on loan servicer practices across the board.

This shouldn't come as a surprise to anyone, though DeVos' particular proclivities for supporting the maximal profits of loan servicers might have become more widely recognized had those Democratic senators been given more than a few minutes to grill DeVos at her confirmation hearing.

---

[57] Nasiripour, S. (3 April 2017). Student Debt Giant Navient to Borrowers: You're on Your Own. *Bloomberg News*. https://www.bloomberg.com/news/articles/2017-04-03/student-debt-giant-navient-to-borrowers-you-re-on-your-own

Among the many financial entanglements DeVos brought with her to Washington, one was a DeVos family investment company named RDV Corporation. RDV was, in turn, tied to the Delaware-based company LMF WF Portfolio I LLC. And *that* confusing series of letters from Delaware was a financial backer of Performant -- a loan collection agency that, at the time, received millions of dollars in Department of Education loan servicing contracts.

Prior to DeVos being tapped as Secretary of Education, this was good business for the family fortune -- the loan servicing company had already received millions of dollars in past Department of Education loan servicing contracts. Every time the company collected on a loan, they took home a commission from the Department of Education. Those commissions provided a little bit of profitable cream for the DeVos family's investment portfolio -- trickle-down economics in the truest sense of the word.

It was a pretty good trickle at that. Performant's 2016 financial report noted that the company had "provided recovery services on approximately $8.6 billion of combined student loans and other delinquent federal and state receivables," including the skip-tracing of defaulted lenders, wage garnishment, and "litigation services." According to a January 2017 Bloomberg report, Performant had a "total revenue of $148.7 million in its most recently reported four quarters," ending in October of 2016. And this money was all coming in at a time when Performant had to compete for Department of Education business amid a sizable of field of firms awarded similar contracts.

Along the way, however, Performant managed to rack up 346 customer complaints with the Better Business Bureau, as well as a healthy share of customer complaints to the Consumer Financial Protection Bureau. It's perhaps not that surprising that in December of 2016, Performant was excluded from a new contract with the Department of Education -- a move that sent Performant's share value down "43 percent in one day," according to Bloomberg.

This all meant that a not-insignificant portion of the DeVos family fortune, knit up in the profits taken by a loan-servicing scofflaw, was lost a few weeks before Trump's inauguration.

Of course the moment DeVos was picked to be Trump's nominee, it triggered a series of mandatory divestitures, in keeping with the guidance offered by the Office of Government Ethics. From an ethical standpoint, such divestments were necessary to prevent potential cabinet members like DeVos from feathering their own nest with the largesse that lucrative government contracts offered. Greg McNeilly, a spokesperson for DeVos, told Bloomberg that she and her husband would, indeed, rid herself of her stake in Performant. However, he did take pains to mention that this would not "obligate other family members or RDV itself to divest" from Performant.

Performant's performance thus still had a role to play in the DeVos family's bankrolls. That puts the steps that the Education Department under DeVos took next in a new light.

DeVos began by defanging the government watchdogs who had traditionally policed the student loan beat, dogging companies like Performant for their failures to properly assist their customers. On April 11, DeVos formally withdrew two memos issued by the Obama administration that offered guidance to the Federal Student Aid office -- responsible for servicing over $1 billion in student loans -- on how to provide better service to borrowers who wanted to manage, or even discharge, their student debt. For the Obama administration it was a late-in-arriving but vital course correction for the agency, which had hitherto acted mainly in the interest of maximizing repayment proceeds.

In June[58], DeVos tapped A. Wayne Johnson, the CEO and founder of a private student loan company named Reunion Financial Services, to run the Department of Education's Federal Student Aid agency.

In Johnson, DeVos would find someone who, like her, had no experience in public education, but an enthusiasm for profiting from it. When the Department of Education announced his appointment, his history at Reunion Financial was conspicuously omitted from his curriculum vitae.

Johnson took the place of James Runcie, who had abruptly resigned in May after scrapping with DeVos over her planned changes to federal student loan programs. "I cannot in good conscience continue to be accountable as Chief Operating Officer given the risk associated with the current environment at the [Education] Department," wrote Runcie in his resignation letter.

Runcie's resignation touched off a wave of chaos and finger-pointing between DeVos, her allies, and congressional Democrats. DeVos partisans intimated that Runcie stepped down in order to avoid a scheduled appearance with the House Oversight Committee on money

---

[58] Greenwood, M. (21 June 2017). DeVos picks CEO of for-profit lender to run federal student loan system. *The Hill*. http://thehill.com/homenews/news/338737-devos-picks-ceo-of-for-profit-lender-to-run-federal-student-loan-system

improperly paid out by the government to loan holders. Runcie, in what would prove to be an unsatisfying denial of this accusation to both congressional overseers and DeVos critics alike, stated only, "I did not leave simply to avoid a hearing on improper payments...That is not credible."

Regardless, Runcie departed under a black cloud. When his agency investigated Navient on the charge that it had systematically overcharged active-duty military loan recipients, it exonerated Navient from wrongdoing -- but a later investigation from the Department of Justice found the FSA's investigation to be, at best, massively incomplete. For example, they failed to account for thousands of violations of federal law. As Nasiripour reported at the time:

> "The Justice Department data on the number of service members overcharged on Education Department-owned loans, previously unreported and provided to HuffPost, underscore a deep divide between the Education Department and Justice Department over how to punish companies accused of violating federal law. It also revives lingering concerns that the Education Department views Navient, a former unit of student loan giant Sallie Mae and one of the nation's largest student loan specialists, as too big to fail."[59]

However, despite all of this, Massachusetts Senator Elizabeth Warren was troubled by Runcie's resignation. Noting that she had had "differences with Jim Runcie's leadership in the past" she nevertheless found "the idea that he would resign amid reports of political meddling from Secretary DeVos" to be "cause for serious alarm."

Navient was, naturally, at the center of the case for "political meddling" as well. It hardly escaped anyone's attention that DeVos' rescinding of those Obama-era memos on student loan protections went a long way toward improving[60] the company's hand in terms of winning a new contract -- or to end up being the sole provider of services in DeVos' vision of a future contracting regime. As Bloomberg reported,

---

[59] Nasiripour, S. (28 April 2014). U.S. Knew Sallie Mae Cheated Service Members On Student Loans, But Still Renewed Contract. *Huffington Post*. https://www.huffingtonpost.com/2014/04/28/sallie-mae-servicemembers_n_5229312.html

[60] Nasiripour, S. (11 April 2017). DeVos Undoes Obama Student Loan Protections. *Bloomberg News*. https://www.bloomberg.com/news/articles/2017-04-11/devos-undoes-obama-student-loan-protections

"Navient shares moved higher after the government released DeVos's decision," ending up "almost 2 percent" on the day. And Navient clearly had plans to expand this aspect of their business: in mid-April, they picked up a $6.9 billion portfolio of student loans from J.P. Morgan.

So there's a logic to Runcie's resignation, though perhaps not one he'd care to admit. It was simply untenable for him to continue in his position, having so badly botched his agency's investigations into Navient's business practices, if Navient -- or any other firm, confident that DeVos was going to allow them to play fast and loose with borrowers' needs -- was just going to emerge later as a big contract winner. As they say: once bitten, twice shy. In A. Wayne Johnson, DeVos had an FSA head that could both claim a slate clean of past controversies, but with the ideological bearing to return Department of Education oversight to the old status quo: profit bundling for corporate servicers, and low bottom lines for agency budgets.

There was just one nagging problem remaining for DeVos: the CFPB. But she would figure out a way to shut them down.

By the middle of the summer, DeVos has abandoned her plan to award a single company the privilege of servicing the entire trillion-dollar student loan kit and kaboodle. Instead she opted to award separate contracts for database housing, system processing and customer service functions to one or more companies possibly handling direct interactions with borrowers, as Inside Higher Ed's Andrew Kreighbaum reported.[61] But she hadn't given up on getting the CFPB's bootheel off the necks of loan servicers, and at the end of August, DeVos would take aim at the information-sharing partnership between the Department of Education and the CFPB, which the consumer protection bureau had used to police the student loan beat so effectively during its brief tenure.

On August 31, Johnson sent a letter to CFPB director Richard Cordray, informing him that the Department of Education intended to terminate the MOU between his agency and the CFPB "regarding the sharing of information in connection with the oversight of student loans." Johnson's central complaint was that the CFPB had "violated the intent" of this memorandum by failing to direct Title IV federal student loan complaints to the Department of Education in a timely enough fashion,

---

[61] Kreighbaum, A. (2 August 2017). DeVos abandons plan to award federal student loan servicing to a single company. *PBS NewsHour*. https://www.pbs.org/newshour/education/devos-abandons-plan-award-federal-student-loan-servicing-single-company

and for expanding the CFPB's "jurisdiction into areas that Congress never envisioned," in reference to the agency's Navient lawsuit.

But what DeVos' Department actually did was officially adopt Navient's line of argument -- that the loan servicer couldn't be reasonably expected to act on behalf of their customers by actively informing them about their options and enrolling them into fairer repayment plans. As Bloomberg reported, the Federal Student Aid office had been "content with low enrollment" in the kinds of plans that allow borrowers to repay at lower rates "until around 2012[62], when the White House and the CFPB began to prod them to direct their contractors to inform eligible borrowers" about them. After this, enrollment "soared."[63]

In other words, the consumer protection bureau was badly gumming up the great profit-raking process, and therefore they needed to be shut down. The artful way Johnson put it in his letter to Cordray was that the CFPB had to be shut out, in order to "enhance the efficiencies of our servicers."

Johnson's letter sprinkled a little creatine all over Wall Street. As Bloomberg's Nasiripour reported, Compass Point research director Michael Tarkan immediately recommended that his clients invest in loan servicing companies. Tarkan said that the Department of Education's letter was an "unambiguous signal" that the Trump administration, and DeVos, was going to be much more accommodating to student loan companies in terms of oversight and scrutiny.

But that would hardly be the only way DeVos would work to Performant's benefit. Not only will this new contract bring the company back into the Department of Education's loan servicer fold after a year of having been cut out entirely, they will be one of only two companies cut in on the Department of Education's student loan portfolio. In the past, the Department has contracted with as many as seventeen firms to perform student loan collection, and as the Washington Post noted, "attempts to whittle down the number of firms have been met with resistance."

Two years ago, when only seven companies were selected to manage the portfolio, it touched off considerable protestations among those companies that were left out of the process -- the January 2018

---

[62] Obama, B. (7 June 2012). Presidential Memorandum--Improving Repayment Options for Federal Student Loan Borrowers. https://obamawhitehouse.archives.gov/the-press-office/2012/06/07/presidential-memorandum-improving-repayment-options-federal-student-loan
[63] Office of Federal Student Aid, U.S. Department of Education. Federal Student Loan Portfolio. https://studentaid.ed.gov/sa/about/data-center/student/portfolio

decision to select new contractors was supposed to resolve this conflict. But DeVos' Department of Education has, perhaps, only re-inflamed this controversy by reducing the field even further: Performant is joined by only one other firm, Windham Professionals, in servicing loan contracts worth an estimated $400 million.

Windham, at the very least, deserved to be dealt in. Back when the field of servicers was reduced to seven firms, protests from the companies that were left out -- including Performant -- forced the Government Accountability Office to undertake a thorough evaluation of all the companies that had submitted bids. According to the GAO's subsequent report, Windham held up quite well in the crowded field, earning an "exceptional" rating for past performance and a "satisfactory" rating for management. Performant, by contrast, did not fare as well -- they only rated "satisfactory" in terms of past performance, and "marginal" on management.

Performant's resurrection has raised eyebrows. As Todd Canni, an attorney for one of the bidders that lost out in the process, told the Washington Post, "It simply does not make sense that the agency would choose to work with lower-rated [companies] with marginal ratings that do not have an exceptional past performance record." Indeed, going just by the GAO's evaluation, there were six other firms besides Windham that rated higher than Performant in the categories of past performance and overall management.

Performant's good news sent their stock price skyrocketing. Meanwhile, spokespersons for everyone involved stepped forward to say the required pleasantries. A Department of Education flack ensured reporters that DeVos had "no knowledge, let alone involvement" in the decision to award Performant the new contract. Richard Zubek, Performant's head of investor relations, followed suit by insisting that no one from the firm "had any direct or indirect contact with Secretary DeVos or anyone related to Mrs. DeVos."

But given Performant's checkered history and mediocre ratings, as well as the existence of substantially higher-rated options among the many companies that had performed loan collection work for the Department of Education, it's difficult to fathom what particular quality allowed Performant to surge back to prominence in the eyes of the Department of Education and to be cut in on more profitable terms this time around. As Canni told the Washington Post, "It is beyond dispute that the [Education Department's] decisions have, at a minimum, created the appearance of a conflict of interest," adding, "Given the fact that

Performant was not a highly rated [company] and, in fact, was rated fairly low...the agency will be under intense scrutiny and will need to explain how suddenly these ratings changed so significantly to allow Performant to leap frog over so many" more deserving firms.

But with the CFPB sidelined, it's not clear from whence this scrutiny will come. What is clear is that the decision is, in any event, going to be good for the DeVos family's business -- providing seed money to Republican office-seekers and the infrastructure of the conservative movement.

Of course, student loan servicers were hardly the only entities receiving clear signals from DeVos that the good times were set to roll anew. Those messages were also very quickly received by another collection of companies, onto whom DeVos planned to lavish new profit-taking privileges: the for-profit education industry.

While the Obama administration spent the bulk of their tenure as reluctant participants in the fight to regulate the for-profit college sector, they eventually left what could be fairly characterized as a virtuous legacy. Their chief accomplishments included two important regulatory reforms. The first was a "gainful employment" rule that would exact a financial penalty on educational institutions -- including for-profit colleges as well as private and public universities -- that were routinely failing to prepare their students to succeed in the workforce.

The second was a "borrower defense" rule that would allow students who could prove that they'd been defrauded or abused by a for-profit entity to cancel their debts to those scofflaw institutions entirely. The rule also banned forced-arbitration proceedings that prevented students from suing fraudulent actors in court.

These reforms were vital protections for students in the for-profit college system as well as the taxpayers whose money partially underwrote these predatory businesses. For-profits were going to have to be accountable for getting their students a good education that put them on a viable career path, instead of selling education gospel snake oil for profit.

For the virtuous actors in the for-profit sector, it provided firmer performance incentives. But for the predatory outfits, these rules promised to be very bad for business. The "gainful employment" rule set rigorous benchmarks for the after-graduation results of students in career programs at both for-profit colleges and public/private universities -- specifically, if a graduate's loan payment was more than 20 percent of their post-graduate discretionary income, or more than 8 percent of their total annual income -- then the institution failed the "gainful employment" test. That meant that out of compliance institutions could find themselves restricted from having their students use federal student loans.

As David Dayen reported for The Nation, the first data set generated by the Department of Education after the gainful employment rule went into effect found that "800 programs serving hundreds of thousands of students" had failed the test. Of these 800 programs, 98 percent were from for-profit colleges. "Because for-profits survive on federal student loans—which make up almost 90 percent of their revenue," wrote Dayen[64], "the regulation is an extremely effective way to put unsuccessful or even predatory for-profits out of business."

It would make sense for an Education Secretary appointed by the titular head of the scammy Trump University to train her guns at these two rules. And indeed DeVos would do all of that and more. By mid-summer, DeVos had gone a considerable way towards getting the government's regulatory bootheel off the necks of for-profit fraudsters.

As you might expect, the DeVos family had extant ties to the industry. Paperwork DeVos provided to the Office of Government Ethics documented family investments in a fund named Avery Point VII CLO, which is connected to a for-profit college megalith Laureate Education, which owns Walden University -- the largest single recipient of federal graduate student loans. DeVos also had $1 million invested in the private equity company named Snow Phipps. As the Center for American Progress reported, Snow Phipps "took Laureate Education private in 2007 and is poised to realize substantial gains once the company goes public again."

Additionally, DeVos' disclosure forms indicated that she has money invested in Apollo Investment Corp., which in turn has its own money invested in Delta Education Systems, which operates 42 for-profit college campuses across the country. As CAP detailed, "According to a spreadsheet[65] of the first official gainful employment results[66] from the Office of Federal Student Aid, Delta has 40 programs at risk of losing

---

[64] Dayen. D. (15 June 2017). Betsy DeVos Moves to Help For-Profit Schools Defraud Students. *The Nation*. https://www.thenation.com/article/betsy-devos-moves-to-help-for-profit-schools-defraud-students/

[65] https://studentaid.ed.gov/sa/sites/default/files/GE-DMYR-2015-Final-Rates.xls

[66] Office of Federal Student Aid, U.S. Department of Education. Gainful Employment Information. https://studentaid.ed.gov/sa/about/data-center/school/ge

access to federal financial aid under the gainful employment regulation."

Moreover, according to a 2006 financial disclosure form filed during Dick DeVos' gubernatorial campaign in Michigan, he and Betsy were pre-IPO investors in a company called K12 Inc., the nation's largest chain of for-profit virtual charter schools. The extent to which the DeVoses' ties to K12 have deepened by the time she was tapped by Trump to lead the Department of Education is unknown, owing to the fact that K12 has no legal obligation to disclose their investors' identities. However, K12's executive chairman, Nate Davis, sure seemed excited by DeVos' ascension into Trump's cabinet, releasing a statement in which he praised her for being "a longtime advocate for strengthening public education and empowering parents with the freedom to choose schools that best meet the needs of their children."

Not that Davis would know much about strengthening public education or meeting the needs of children. As Buzzfeed's Molly Hensley-Clancy reported[67], K12's record in that regard was so threadbare that its own investors took the company to task at its December 2015 shareholders meeting, voting against the company's planned payouts to executives due to a "substantial disconnect between compensation and performance results." Outside the meeting, a gathering of protesters "accused one of the company's largest school networks, the California Virtual Academies (CAVA), of failing its 15,000 students." Their complaints were not without merit. A 2015 report[68] from Washington, D.C. research firm In The Public Interest found that CAVA had generated "more high school dropouts than graduates while collecting attendance funds for students who log in for one minute a day, or don't participate at all."

K12 can probably credit its continued existence to its political connections. As PR Watch's Dustin Beilke reported, K12 managed to buy themselves a seat on the corporate board of the American Legislative Executive Council (ALEC), "where for years it has[d] also paid for a seat and vote on ALEC's 'Education and Workforce Development' Task Force.

[67] Hensley-Clancy, M. (16 December 2015). Investors Rebel Against Controversial Online School Operator K12. *BuzzFeed News*. https://www.buzzfeed.com/mollyhensleyclancy/investors-rebel-against-controversial-online-school-operator?utm_term=.yn6K6awq3#.ecpx58z0b

[68] Adams, J. (26 February 2015). Report alleges poor academics at for-profit virtual schools. *EdSource*. https://edsource.org/2015/report-alleges-poor-academics-at-for-profit-virtual-schools/75329

Per Beilke:

> ALEC corporations spend tens of thousands of dollars each year for such access to lawmakers, and K12 has also paid many thousands of dollars to underwrite some of ALEC's docket of events for legislators and lobbyists.

> Through the ALEC Task Force, K12 has actually had an equal vote with state legislators on so-called "model" bills to divert taxpayer funds away from traditional public schools toward the objectives of ALEC's private sector funders, to help their bottom-lines and/or legislative agenda.

> ALEC's "Virtual Public Schools Act," for example, even allows virtual schools to be paid the same amount per pupil as traditional public schools even though operations like K12 have no bricks and mortar school house or desks or air-conditioning or gyms, etc., to maintain.[69]

It's easy to see how a company like K12 fits snugly within DeVos' ideological worldview. Here we have an outfit whose efforts to advance their profit-taking mission and ideological agenda run in inverse proportion to the level of competence demonstrated at its core educational mission. If anything, this is the DeVos philosophy, distilled to its high-proof dose. One can easily imagine how K12 officials thought that having DeVos running the Department of Ed might pay dividends down the road. If anything, though, DeVos would go on to demonstrate a willingness to spread the wealth around considerably -- with predatory for-profit colleges representing one huge beneficiary.

If DeVos' own connections to the for-profit education industry weren't enough of a clue as to her intentions, the people with whom she swiftly selected to surround herself left no doubt. In March, DeVos hired Robert Eitel to serve as a special adviser; Eitel had previously served as the vice president for regulatory legal services for the for-profit operator Bridgepoint Education. As the New York Times reported[70], during Eitel's

---

[69] Center for Media and Democracy. Virtual Public Schools Act Exposed. https://www.alecexposed.org/w/images/4/4a/2D23-Virtual_Public_Schools_Act1_Exposed.pdf

[70] Cohen, P. (17 March 2017). Betsy DeVos's Hiring of For-Profit College Official Raises Impartiality Issues. The New York Times. https://www.nytimes.com/2017/03/17/business/education-for-profit-robert-eitel.html?_r=0

tenure at Bridgepoint, he had considerable opportunity to put his legal skills to the test, as the company endured "multiple government investigations, including one that ended with a settlement of more than $30 million over deceptive student lending." Prior to his time at Bridgepoint, Eitel was a lawyer within President George W. Bush's Education Department, where he was a noted critic of efforts to regulate the for-profit education sector. (A department spokesperson promised that Eitel would recuse himself from decisions affecting his former employer, though how that promise would be enforced wasn't made clear.)

In August, another fox was brought in to guard the for-profit henhouse when Julian Schmoke was hired[71] to head up the Department of Education's enforcement division -- the team that would be chiefly responsible for investigating claims of fraud and wrongdoing. While Schmoke didn't bring much in the way of investigative or enforcement expertise to the position, he was at least capable of appreciating the matter from the other side. His previous employer, for-profit institution DeVry University, could boast of having been, at one time or another, under multiple investigations[72] from the Department of Education, the Justice Department, the Department of Veterans' Affairs, and three states' attorneys general. In December of 2016, DeVry agreed to a $100 million settlement[73] with the Federal Trade Commission after the FTC sued the company for misleading prospective students with deceptive advertisements.

Carlos Muniz, who President Trump chose to serve as the Department of Education's general counsel, was also an anthropomorphic red flag. Muniz came to the Department fresh from serving as a lawyer at McGuireWoods, where he provided nebulous "consulting services" to for-profit education company Career Education Corp., which also faced "multiple state investigations." But if anything, he's probably best known as having been a top aide to Florida AG Pam Bondi during the period when she famously decided to not pursue legal

---

[71] Berman, J. (30 August 2017). Trump admin reportedly hires a former for-profit college dean for fraud enforcement. *MarketWatch*. https://www.marketwatch.com/story/trump-admin-reportedly-hires-a-former-for-profit-college-dean-for-fraud-enforcement-2017-08-30

[72] Halperin, D. (7 March 2018). Law Enforcement Investigations and Actions Regarding For-Profit Colleges. *Republic Report*. https://www.republicreport.org/2014/law-enforcement-for-profit-colleges/

[73] Federal Trade Commission. (15 December 2016). DeVry University Agrees to $100 Million Settlement with FTC. https://www.ftc.gov/news-events/press-releases/2016/12/devry-university-agrees-100-million-settlement-ftc

action against Trump University after $25,000 of Trump Foundation money found its way into a pro-Bondi PAC. As the Associated Press reported[74], emails showed that Muniz "was included in discussions about student complaints alleging fraud" with Trump University.

DeVos also briefly employed Taylor Hansen, a former lobbyist for Career Education Colleges and Universities (CECU), the largest trade group for the for-profit college industry. Hansen worked on what the Department of Education referred to as DeVos' "beach-head team" -- a small cabal of temporary hires with the broad power to set policy, but who could escape the rigors of Senate confirmation. Hansen's work up to that point had chiefly been concerned with eliminating the gainful employment rule. Soon after ProPublica reported on his presence on this team, Senator Elizabeth Warren sent a letter to DeVos seeking further information on his hiring. Warren wrote that, "Mr. Hansen's recent employment history clearly calls into question his impartiality in dealing with higher education issues at the Department of Education, and raises alarming conflicts of interest concerns." Rather than answer to those concerns, Hansen departed the agency. "He served ably and without conflict and decided his service had run its course," said a spokesperson.

That DeVos took these people into her inner circle, even temporarily, spoke volumes about how she'd regulate the often unruly wilderness of for-profit education. But soon enough, she was speaking through her actions.

On June 14, DeVos pulled the trigger, announcing[75] that the gainful employment rule and the borrower defense rule (which was set to go into effect on July 1) would be put on hold and radically rewritten, thus stalling all of these protections that students who had been victimized by for-profit colleges had already started to use in their own defense. DeVos also shut down an interagency task force that had been set up during the Obama administration to conduct oversight over the for-profit sector. While no significant enforcement activity had been conducted during this task force's brief life, Inside Higher Ed reported that "the task force was key to promoting cooperation between both federal agencies and state

---

[74] Biesecker, M., Fineout, G. (12 April 2017). Trump taps lawyer involved with Trump U case for federal job. *Associated Press*. https://apnews.com/4e4eaba253164b9e88c8f67de504d4d8/trump-taps-lawyer-involved-trump-u-case-federal-job

[75] U.S. Department of Education. (14 June 2017). Secretary DeVos Announces Regulatory Reset to Protect Students, Taxpayers, Higher Ed Institutions. https://www.ed.gov/news/press-releases/secretary-devos-announces-regulatory-reset-protect-students-taxpayers-higher-ed-institutions

attorneys general" so that this beat could be policed in a coordinated manner.

In a July 2017 speech to members of ALEC, DeVos made it clear that she would be moving to gut the Obama-era reforms of the for-profit college industry, specifically referencing the borrower defense and gainful employment rules as "textbook overreach" done "solely to advance their administration-wide war on every type of organization they didn't like."

"The uncomfortable truth for those rule-makers," she added, "was that if many traditional institutions were held to the same standards as for-profit entities, many of them would fail the Gainful Employment requirements too." Not quite. As The Institute for College Access and Success pointed out[76], the gainful employment rule "covers more public programs than [for-profit programs], and no public programs failed."

Nevertheless, DeVos characterized her moves as a "regulatory reset," and spoke euphemistically about considering the needs of students. "While students should have protection from predatory practices, schools should also be treated fairly," she proclaimed. A nice sentiment, to be sure, but DeVos' talk would prove to be awfully cheap compared to her actions, all of which essentially put the finger on the scales in ways that consistently favored the for-profit privateers. Time and again, DeVos -- no doubt influenced heavily by the plethora of cronies she'd surrounded herself with -- found new and more innovative ways to ensure that the for-profit education industry would receive gold-star treatment from the Department of Ed. Meanwhile, the students would consistently get the shaft.

By the end of July, DeVos' agency had stopped approving any applications for student-loan forgiveness under the borrower defense rule. The shutdown only came to light[77] after records pertaining to the ED's processing of claimant applications found their way into the hands of Senator Dick Durbin, a Democrat from Illinois. In addition to halting application approvals, Durbin discovered that DeVos' Department of Ed had also stopped processing student loan relief for tens of thousands of borrowers. This backlog of 65,000 claims included students who'd been defrauded by for-profits like Corinthian and ITT Technical Schools.

---

[76] The Institute for College Access and Success. (20 July 2017). "Hmm. 3 federal courts fully upheld the reg, it's 19 FR pages, it covers more public programs than #4profit, and no public programs failed." https://twitter.com/TICAS_org/status/888134972057550848

[77] Binkley, C. (26 July 2017). Records: Student-loan forgiveness has halted under Trump. *Associated Press.* https://apnews.com/f472a4ef9a3b4b3dbdeb2ca353b9f65e

Moreover, the borrowers waiting for their extant claims to be processed by the Education Department were still accruing loan interest -- to the tune of $154 million -- as well as facing the end of their temporarily permitted loan forbearance periods.

In August, the Department of Education announced that it would be taking a stronger approach to enforcing compliance by institutions participating in federal student aid programs "by creating stronger consumer protections for students, parents and borrowers against 'bad actors.'" In its announcement, DeVos -- asserting that "protecting students has always been my top priority" -- promised a "new approach" that would "enhance" those efforts through a process of "executive outreach to ensure parties and their leadership understand their responsibilities, the consequences of non-compliance and appropriate remedies."

Experts saw quickly through the cheap talk. As Century Foundation fellow Bob Shireman told Inside Higher Ed[78], "If colleges know that the Department of Education will always warn them politely and secretly when they are caught ripping off students and taxpayers, bad actors have little reason to steer clear of predatory recruiting practices. The approach is a recipe for disaster: it encourages fraud and abuse and is exactly the attitude that allowed the massive consumer abuses in the early 2000s and through the recession."

Indeed, in practice, the DeVos approach was to grant reprieves to such bad actors. One beneficiary of DeVos' forgiveness was the for-profit Charlotte School of Law, which had been sanctioned under the previous administration for its continual failure to meet compliance requirements[79] set by the American Bar Association, its accreditor. "The ABA repeatedly found that the Charlotte School of Law does not prepare students for participation in the legal profession. Yet CSL continuously misrepresented itself to current and prospective students as hitting the mark," said then-U.S. Under Secretary of Education Ted Mitchell in a statement.

---

[78] Shireman, R. (31 August 2017). Statement of Robert Shireman, Senior Fellow, The Century Foundation, in response to U.S. Department of Education Announcement about Consumer Protection in Higher Education.
https://drive.google.com/file/d/0B7adHdBE6w3meW9jQjVfM2xLUWc/view
[79] Nasiripour, S. (2 August 2017). DeVos Offers a Lifeline to For-Profit Law School That Hired Her Former Adviser. Bloomberg News. https://www.bloomberg.com/news/articles/2017-08-02/devos-offers-a-lifeline-to-for-profit-law-school-that-hired-her-former-adviser

Despite these findings -- and the fact that North Carolina's attorney general had announced[80] that his office was launching further investigation into the school's practices in April of 2017 -- DeVos' Department of Ed re-opened the floodgates, granting CSL access to taxpayer money on a conditional basis.[81] It probably helped that the beleaguered school was able to secure the services of Podesta Group lobbyist Lauren Maddox[82] -- the same woman who was hired to shepherd DeVos through the confirmation process.

In December of 2016, the Department of Education cut off[83] Globe University and the Minnesota School of Business -- ventures owned and operated by for-profit college kingpin Terry Myhre -- from access to federal student aid programs after a Minnesota court found them guilty of fraud and deceptive trade practices. As the Minneapolis Star-Tribune reported[84], Globe's misdeeds had been previously exposed by a former dean-turned-whistleblower who Globe fired for complaining about her employer's "unethical practices." These practices included "deceptive job-placement rates for its graduates, and giving false assurances that its credits would transfer to other colleges." In her successful suit against Globe[85], Minnesota AG Lori Swanson proved that the same practices were being deployed to dupe graduates of the chain's criminal justice program.

The Myhre family's solution to their problem was to simply shut down operations in Minnesota, and sell Globe's Wisconsin-based campuses to another for-profit chain they owned, Broadview University.

---

[80] Worley, H., Liles, M. (12 April 2017). Letter to Betsy DeVos Regarding Charlotte School of Law. *Department of Justice, State of North Carolina*.
http://media2.newsobserver.com/content/media/2017/4/28/2017.04.12%20Ltr%20to%20Betsy%20DeVos%20re%20CSL.PDF

[81] Frola, M. (27 July 2017). Re: Conditions for Application for Reinstatement for Participation in Title IV Programs. *Office of Federal Student Aid, U.S. Department of Education*.
http://www.abajournal.com/files/Charlotte_Conditions_for_Reinstatment.pdf

[82] Nasiripour, S. (2 August 2017). DeVos Offers a Lifeline to For-Profit Law School That Hired Her Former Adviser. *Bloomberg News*. https://www.bloomberg.com/news/articles/2017-08-02/devos-offers-a-lifeline-to-for-profit-law-school-that-hired-her-former-adviser

[83] U.S. Department of Education. (6 December 2016). Globe University, Minnesota School of Business Denied Access to Federal Student Aid Dollars. https://www.ed.gov/news/press-releases/globe-university-minnesota-school-business-denied-access-federal-student-aid-dollars

[84] Lerner, M. (19 April 2015). Globe U whistleblower collects as school battles Minnesota AG, falling enrollment. http://www.startribune.com/globe-u-whistleblower-collects-as-school-battles-minnesota-ag-falling-enrollment/300553531/?c=y&page=all&prepage=1#continue

[85] Office of the Minnesota Attorney General. Amended Complaint Against Minnesota School of Business and Globe University.
http://media.graytvinc.com/documents/Globe_Amended_Complaint_(3_8_15+redlined).pdf

The Obama administration blocked[86] this move on the grounds that the two chains' common ownership suggested that the same bad practices would simply continue in a new venue. But DeVos reversed that Obama-era decision[87], and the Myhre family hydra simply grew a new head.

These were institutions that, by any standard, should have been left for dead, with only the memories of the harm wrought by their predatory practices lingering afterwards. But here they are, alive and well, flowering in a newly-revived laissez-faire environment ripe for continued abuse.

All of the miracle-working that DeVos has lavished upon some of the biggest crooks in the for-profit industry stands in stark contrast to the students whose needs she has promised to keep in balance. In DeVos' Department of Education, these students couldn't even gain an audience. And so, finding themselves locked out of the remedies that the Obama administration had hoped to create for them, and with the Department of Education no longer playing any sort of role in policing the for-profit sector, it fell to others to seek redress for victims in the only remaining venue -- the courts.

Over the past year, lawyers from the Harvard Law School Legal Services Center's Project on Predatory Student Lending have filed four-high profile suits against DeVos and the Department of Education, each of which highlights the shabby treatment students received from the federal government. In each case, the plaintiffs had compelling claims and could prove they'd been victimized by programs that had systematically violated laws -- all of which the Department of Education was empowered -- indeed, obligated -- to remedy. Yet in every instance, it was the victims of for-profit fraud that ended up getting punished.

- **Williams vs. DeVos:** Darnell Williams and Yessenia Taveras, both of whom attended the Everest Institute -- a subsidiary of the defunct Corinthian Colleges chain -- in Massachusetts, have filed suit in federal court, challenging the Department of Education's right to continue to seize their money to pay off their defaulted student loan. Williams and Taveras, who each attended career programs at Everest, each had their federal tax refunds seized by the Department despite the fact that Corinthian had been shut

[86] U.S. Department of Education. (6 December 2016). Denial of Recertification of Globe University. https://studentaid.ed.gov/sa/sites/default/files/globe-recert-denial.pdf

[87] Fain, P. (9 August 2017). A Shuttered For-Profit Re-emerges. *Inside Higher Ed.* https://www.insidehighered.com/news/2017/08/09/wisconsin-profit-re-emerges-backing-state-and-trump-administration

down after being accused of widespread, systemic fraud. The Harvard lawyers contend that the Department of Education had no legal right to seize their clients' money due to Corinthian's fraudulent practices -- of which the Department was fully aware at the time of the seizure.

- **Dieffenbacher vs. DeVos:** Sarah Dieffenbacher, who also attended a school in the Corinthian network in California, has sued the Department of Education for continuing to garnish her wages to repay student loan debt that should have been legally cancelled because the program she attended -- a paralegal training program offered by Everest College-Ontario Metro -- violated California law. According to the suit, officials at Everest "lied to [Dieffenbacher] about her job prospects after attending, its career assistance, its program quality and career training, the transferability and usefulness of its credits, and its program cost," all while leaving her $50,000 in debt and "unable to find a job she had trained for." Dieffenbacher had contacted the Department of Education on four separate occasions, requesting that her debt be cancelled, citing her legal right and the school's known misconduct, only to receive no response prior to the Department suddenly seizing her wages.

- **Colon vs. DeVos:** Tina Carr and Yvette Colon filed suit against the Department of Education and Navient on the grounds that their continued collection of their student loans is unlawful. The two women, both former students of Sanford-Brown -- an institution owned by the Career Education Corporation chain of for-profit schools -- were deceived at every turn by program officials, who lied about their school's accreditation and track record. The attorney general of New York, in his own probe of CEC, had by this time "found that CEC systematically cheated students like Ms. Carr and Ms. Colon," by citing fraudulent job placement statistics and failing to disclose the fact that their credits could not be transferred "to legitimate schools," among other violations of the state's consumer protection laws.

- **Challenge To Borrower Defense Delay:** Harvard's Project on Predatory Student Lending has also challenged DeVos' decision to delay the implementation of the borrower defense rule on behalf of two plaintiffs, Meaghan Bauer and Stephano Del Rose, former students of EDMC-owned New England Institute of Art. Both students, according to the Harvard lawyers, are "counting on" the provision of the borrower defense rule that "prohibits schools receiving federal funds from relying on forced arbitration agreements with their students," so that they might "have their day in court."

In July, this particular legal pursuit of DeVos escalated, when attorneys general from 18 states and the District of Columbia sued the Department of Education over the delay of the borrower defense rule, asking a U.S. district court to force its implementation. In their complaint, these attorneys general cited the fact that their states had collectively pursued "numerous costly and time-intensive investigations and enforcement actions against proprietary and for-profit schools" which had violated consumer protection statutes. The AGs accused DeVos and her agency of purposefully dragging their feet in order to shield these scofflaws from accountability.

In a statement, Massachusetts Attorney General Maura Healey offered a withering assessment of DeVos' actions. "Since Day 1, Secretary DeVos has sided with for-profit school executives against students and families drowning in unaffordable student loans. Her decision to cancel vital protections for students and taxpayers is a betrayal of her office's responsibility and a violation of federal law. We call on Secretary DeVos and the U.S. Department of Education to restore these rules immediately."

In October, a similar legal action[88] undertaken by 18 state attorneys general targeted DeVos for delaying the implementation of the gainful employment rule. A spokesperson for the Department of Education subsequently decried the suits as frivolous legal stunts, but it's worth pointing out that during the entire time that DeVos and her underlings delayed the implementation, their oft-spoken promises to do right by the students who had already begun the process of seeking a remedy for their claims went conspicuously unfulfilled.

---

[88] Thomsen, J. (17 October 2017). 18 Dem AGs sue DeVos for blocking Obama for-profit college rule. *The Hill*. http://thehill.com/homenews/administration/355885-18-dem-ags-sue-devos-for-blocking-obama-for-profit-college-rule

As Buzzfeed's Hensley-Clancy reported[89] at the time of the second lawsuit, "The Education Department has yet to approve a single claim by a defrauded student under DeVos's watch." A week later, when DeVos had concocted yet another delay in the implementation of the borrower defense rule, the Washington Post's report[90] reiterated this point:

> There are over 87,000 applications for debt relief pending at the department, according to people within the agency who were not authorized to speak publicly. At least 10,000 of those claims have been recommended for approval, but people familiar with the matter say department officials are refusing to pull the trigger.

At the end of September, an occasion for DeVos to actually meet some of the victims of predatory for-profit colleges arose when she traveled to Boston to attend a two-day conference on charter schools and school vouchers, hosted by Harvard's Kennedy School of Government. DeVos was scheduled to speak at this event. Massachusetts Attorney General Healey joined with Harvard's Project on Predatory Lending, asking DeVos to meet with some of the students that stood to be adversely affected by all the policy changes she was promising to unleash.

In a letter, the Project on Predatory Lending's Toby Merrill and Eileen Connor reminded DeVos that she had the power to cancel the debts of the victims of fraudulent practices, and urged her to "sit down and meet with these students" while she was visiting Harvard. Merrill and Connor lamented that DeVos and her Department had "gone out of its way to side with the predatory for-profit college industry, and against students and taxpayers," despite their "reprehensible behavior."

Merrill and Connor continued:

> For instance, just this month, your Department chose to flout a court order, and further delay a decision to cancel the student

---

[89] Hensley, Clancy, M. (17 October 2017). Betsy DeVos Is Being Sued By 17 States Over For-Profit College Rules. *BuzzFeed News*. https://www.buzzfeed.com/mollyhensleyclancy/17-states-and-dc-are-suing-betsy-devos-over-for-profit?utm_term=.hd7037zVj#.taBanGoMW

[90] Douglas-Gabriel, D. (24 October 2017). DeVos calls for another delay of rule to protect students from predatory colleges. *Washington Post*. https://www.washingtonpost.com/news/grade-point/wp/2017/10/24/devos-calls-for-another-delay-of-rule-to-protect-students-from-predatory-colleges/?utm_term=.5288739f0eec

loans of Sarah Dieffenbacher, a hardworking mother of four who was defrauded by Everest College. Instead of cancelling Sarah's loans as the law requires, your Department has instead repeatedly threatened to garnish her wages and take her tax refunds. The federal court characterized your Department's behavior as "frivolous and in bad faith."

In July, your Department also chose to delay the implementation of critical new rules that would protect students and level the playing field for those seeking loan relief. These duly promulgated rules would have gone into effect on July 1 under the normal course. Instead, your Department took the extraordinary step of delaying these new protections and tilting the playing field back toward for-profit colleges. Not only was the Department's action wrong, it was illegal.

These are two of the many decisions that your Department has made that have so negatively impacted these former students. We can arrange for former students to meet with you at the University prior to or following your remarks. In light of your access to the perspectives of the many industry insiders you have hired to work at the Department, it is critical that you hear from these students who have been so harmed by this predatory industry. We hope you can make the time.

As you might suspect, those hopes were dashed. DeVos declined the invitation to meet for just a few hours with the students that were on the other side of the issue. "I'm disappointed that she refused to meet with our clients," Merrill told the Washington Post[91], "but not completely surprised given how frequently the department has sided with industry over students."

The federal government, with DeVos at the helm of the Education Department, may be on the sidelines when it comes to regulating the industry, but there are always the states, right?

---

[91] Douglas-Gabriel, D. (28 September 2017). DeVos rejects invitation to meet with former for-profit college students. *Washington Post*. https://www.washingtonpost.com/news/grade-point/wp/2017/09/28/devos-rejects-invitation-to-meet-with-former-for-profit-college-students/?utm_term=.56c3099e0760

Indeed, because of what loan servicers have been up to in recent years, states around the country have begun suing the loan companies and passing new consumer protections laws.

The very thought offends the sensibilities of Betsy DeVos. Over the winter, word leaked out –- to, again, Bloomberg's Nasiripour -- that the Education Department was considering implementing a rule that would bar states from taking services to court, or regulating their activity in any way.

She didn't have the authority to issue such a rule, and members of both party decried the move as needlessly cruel and an overreach of her power. Yet in March, she went forward with it anyway, dropping into the federal register what she called an "interpretation" of the authority states had to police student loan companies. Her interpretation was a simple one: they had no authority at all, she deemed.

Instead, only the federal government could regulate them, and don't worry, she was going to get around to that at any moment.

One official inside the Consumer Financial Protection Bureau noted how similar the move was to Bush administration efforts to block states from regulating mortgage providers in the run-up to the bank meltdown. "She is recreating the conditions that led to the financial crisis," he said. "Maybe I'm too close to this, but I feel like this is one of those 'what did you do when this happened' moments."

Randi Weingarten, head of the American Federation of Teachers, reacted with unusually strong language when The Intercept reported that DeVos had, despite the outcry, gone ahead with issuing her interpretation. "With this move, she has castrated any state legislators and attorneys general from providing meaningful oversight of student loan services, yet she continues to fail to do so herself," she said.

But there was one voice that sang a different tune than the chorus of opposition. It came deep from the gut, a belted-out melody that rang out in the Calvinist skies above. It came from the National Council of Higher Education Resources –- the lobby group that represents the student loan servicer industry. "NCHER and its membership have long believed that the federal student loan programs –- both the Federal Direct Loan Program and the Federal Family Education Loan Program –- are national in scope and need to be administered uniformly throughout the 50 states," said James Bergeron, the group's president.

The student loan industry's prayers had been answered.

An interesting thing to consider: Betsy DeVos would have probably ended up playing a key role, perhaps even serving as the Secretary of Education, in any of the administrations of the Republicans who ran for president in 2016. But ending up as a creature in Donald Trump's swamp may have been the best possible outcome for her.

Much of what DeVos has done in her career, she's done noisily. When her political footprint landed in Michigan, it hit with a clatter and bang on the landscape, and her unleashed transformations of the Great Lakes State have been controversial and polarizing. The failure of her specifically envisioned charter school system in that state has also garnered a lot of attention, and many in the "education reform" movement -- charter school proponents, voucher mavens, modern-day "disruptors" -- prefer to keep their distance from DeVos, cognizant of the fact that she doesn't reflect well. And she's nothing if not brash -- she's made it clear that she believes that the Republican donor class is entitled to front-of-the-line consideration whenever Capitol Hill legislators turn their attention to crafting policy.

But the Trump administration's ability to draw the media's attention to whatever daily dysfunction is happening close to the Oval Office has largely helped keep the heat off of DeVos. In a normal, more even-tempered administration, many of her decisions -- appointments shrouded in comical conflicts of interest, the tearing-down of guidelines that protect students from harm, her obvious preference for maximizing the lucre of for-profit predators -- might have been bigger stories. In a more even-keeled Cabinet, the way that polls have continually revealed an extremity of public distrust for her might have inspired a more meticulous examination from the press.

But in Trump's Washington, they barely even merit attention. How can such complicated-to-tell stories compete against the hour-by-hour reality-show spectacle of the Trump White House? DeVos has been untouched by these regularly scheduled cable-news embarrassments. And so, in an administration that can boast an untold level of staff turnover, she remains, quietly ensconced at the Department of Education, largely out of sight and out of mind, working her way deftly -- as she always has -- toward limiting protections for the most vulnerable students in America, while allowing the privateers growing fat off the land of income inequality to haul in a greater and greater share of profits. People largely regard her as an idiot, but she's been busy -- and effective. And she may be around for a long time.

ABOUT THE AUTHORS

Jason Linkins

Jason Linkins is a senior editor at ThinkProgress. Previously, he was a founding member of the Huffington Post's Washington, DC bureau. His work has appeared at The Baffler, NBC News, Maclean's, and DCist. Chances are good he's listening to the Replacements right at this very moment.

Phil Lewis

Phil Lewis is a front page editor at HuffPost. A graduate of Michigan State University and Wayne State University's College of Education, he taught in Detroit before working in journalism. He is an avid Vernors drinker.

Made in the USA
San Bernardino, CA
19 March 2018